DATE DUE OCT 0 3

NOV 0 8 '05	NOV 2 9 2004		
GAYLORD			PRINTED IN U.S.A.

B

KICK BOXING

Eddie Cave

THE LYONS PRESS

Guilford, Connecticut
An Imprint of the Globe Pequot Press

DISCLAIMER

AUTHOR'S ACKNOWLEDGMENTS

I would like to thank all my kickboxing colleagues who gave me their support and advice while I was writing this book. Special thanks to the team at New Holland Publishers: the designer, Geraldine Cupido; the editor, Simon Lewis and commissioning editor, Simon Pooley, for all their help and friendliness. I also thank my wife, Wilna, who inspired and motivated me throughout the time it took to work on this book.

MESSAGE FROM DR ENNIO FALSONI
(World President of the World Association of Kickboxing Organizations, WAKO)

I salute this book by Eddie Cave – a wise, old karateka who, like a monk, knows the spiritual truth: train hard, observe the basics in your kickboxing style and you will have a future. This is the simple message contained in this book that I recommend to everybody, newcomers to the sport and experts alike.

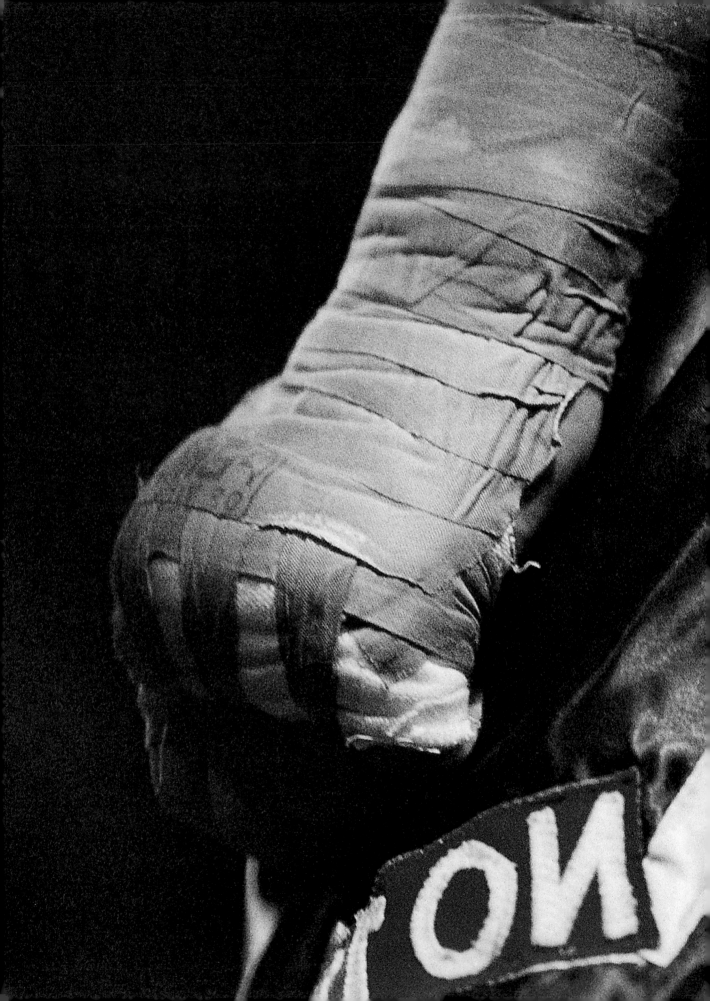

CONTENTS

I NTRODUCTION

Modern kickboxing

Joe Lewis, the first Professional Karate Association (PKA) World Heavyweight Kickboxing Champion, was a pioneer of full-contact karate and fought in the prototype full-contact bout in Long Beach, California in January 1970. It was Lewis who contacted karate innovator Mike Anderson with a view to organizing and promoting the new sport of full-contact

karate, as it was called in those days. Full-contact karate, now called kickboxing, was officially born in Los Angeles in September 1974 when Anderson, together with Don and Judy Quine, formed the first world sanctioning body for the new sport and named it the PKA. They then promoted the first full-contact World Professional Karate Championships, which saw the Americans Joe Lewis, Bill Wallace and Jeff Smith claiming world titles.

This was the beginning of modern kickboxing. By 1975 Bill 'Superfoot' Wallace had become the first superstar of full-contact kickboxing. Another world champion, Benny 'The Jet' Urquidez from the USA, promoted kickboxing by travelling to countries all over the world, including Asia, and then beating their best kickboxers in their own home towns under their rules.

Kickboxing spreads to Europe

George Bruckner from Germany, who was a close friend of Mike Anderson, pioneered full-contact karate in Europe. In 1975 Bruckner, together with other European martial artists, formed the World All Style Karate Organization (WAKO). Bruckner worked extremely hard to advertise and promote the sport of kickboxing all over Europe and promoted the first European Kickboxing Championships in Germany in 1976.

In 1978, Bruckner promoted the first WAKO World Championships in West Berlin, with 18 countries competing. Full-contact karate, or kickboxing, was by this time spreading globally and had become an international sport. Whereas the Americans had considered only the professional aspect of kickboxing, WAKO (which changed its name to the World Association of Kickboxing Organizations) is the world's leading amateur kickboxing organization. WAKO conducts kickboxing competitions in semi-, light- and full-contact, as

opposite SOUTH AFRICAN MIKE BARNADO IS THE WORLD HEAVY-WEIGHT MUAY THAI CHAMPION. HE IS ALSO THE WORLD BOXING FEDERATION (WBF) HEAVYWEIGHT CHAMPION AND THE FIRST HEAVYWEIGHT TO WIN A WORLD KICKBOXING AND A WORLD BOXING TITLE. MIKE FIRST GAINED INTERNATIONAL FAME WHEN HE KNOCKED OUT STAN 'THE MAN' LONGINES IN THE K-1 THAI BOXING CHAMPIONSHIP IN TOKYO IN 1995.

top TWO MALE KICKBOXERS DURING A FULL-CONTACT BOUT.

above left TWO FEMALE KICKBOXERS IN A LIGHT-CONTACT BOUT.

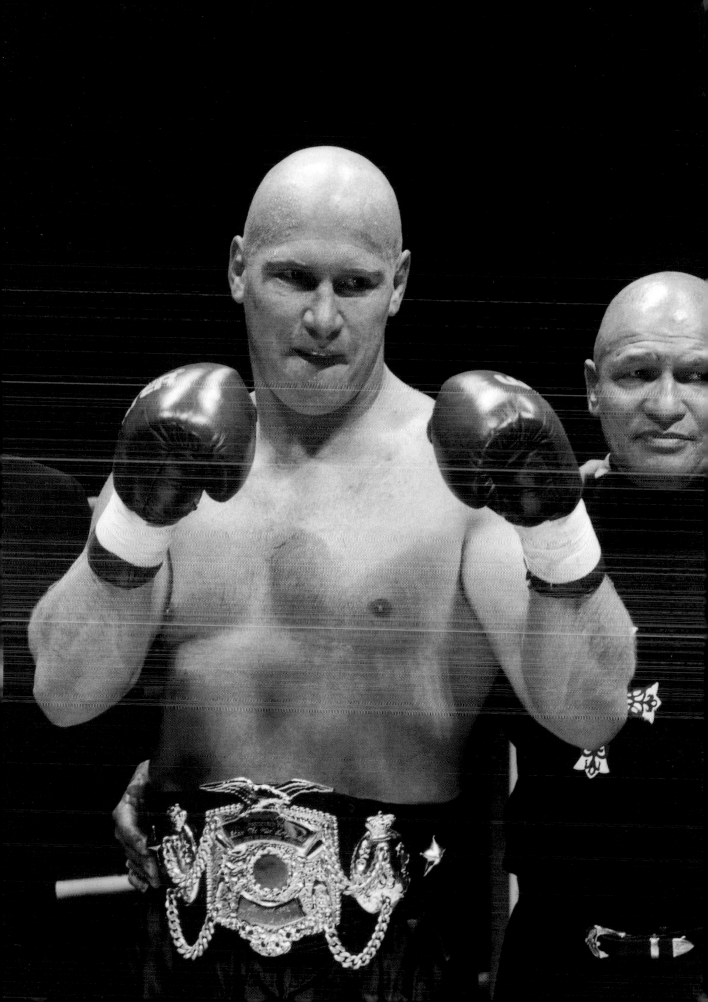

well as musical and weapon forms. The organization's headquarters are in Milan, Italy, under the direction of the World President, Dr Ennio Falsoni.

In the USA, a number of other world kickboxing sanctioning bodies came into being, namely the WKA (World Karate Association), ISKA (International Sport Karate Association), KICK (Karate International Council of Kickboxing), PKC (Professional Karate Commission) and WAKO-Pro (World Association of Kickboxing Organizations — Professional). With the formation of these sanctioning bodies, promoters in the USA and elsewhere began to promote world title fights as well as international kickboxing bouts.

Kickboxing had started to gain in popularity all over the world, to the point where it had become both an internationally recognized sport and martial arts discipline.

TWO THAI BOXERS IN ACTION DURING A BOUT. THE FIGHTER ON THE RIGHT IS EXECUTING A ROUNDHOUSE KICK TO HIS OPPONENT'S BODY.

They discovered that they were not as fit or conditioned as they had thought and they struggled to fight 10 rounds in the professional ring. As a result they tired easily and lost their techniques and the fights became scrappy affairs. The full-contact fighters also discovered to their dismay that their punches and kicks were not as effective in the ring as they had expected. This was largely due to the fact that traditional martial artists are trained to pull back their punches and kicks instead of driving them in with impact and force.

In order to develop kickboxing and to improve the sport, kickboxers turned to the training, conditioning and fighting techniques of western professional boxing. Boxers sparred for countless rounds in preparation for their bouts. Their sparring was virtually full-contact and they took hundreds of punches to the body and head during sparring. This toughened, conditioned and tempered their bodies and strengthened their minds and will. They became mentally and physically prepared to do battle every time they entered the ring. They also developed their punching power by hitting the heavy bag and the jab pads every day.

The pioneer full-contact karate fighters therefore went to the boxing gyms and learned all the secrets of the fight game, sparring with boxers and being trained under boxing trainers.

Boxing training techniques and strategies were therefore incorporated into and adopted by the sport of kickboxing. Kickboxers began to improve tremendously and their techniques became more powerful as they became much fitter and better conditioned than ever before. The kickboxing bouts became more action-packed and exciting. The dynamic modern version of kickboxing had arrived on the internationally sport circuit and was expanding and spreading all over the world.

Development of kickboxing

When full-contact karate (now kickboxing) first began as a sport in the USA in the early seventies, the fighters of that time had to learn through a process of trial and error. The fighters all came from the ranks of traditional karate or other traditional martial arts, and when they fought in professional full-contact bouts certain shortcomings and defects became apparent.

Kickboxing today

Modern kickboxing has a market estimated to have around one million participants in some 6000 clubs around the globe. Today, over 25,000 professional kickboxers worldwide compete in this full-contact sport. Numerous people all over the world use the training as personal fitness regime and, indeed, regard it as the ultimate workout. Today's kickboxers are stronger and fitter, faster and better conditioned than ever before due to improved, modern scientific training techniques, as well as the equipment and facilities now available to them. This dynamic fighting art continues to expand and grow rapidly in popularity.

Benefits of kickboxing

Not only does kickboxing teach valuable self-defence techniques and quicken the reflexes, it also appeals because of the intense and revolutionary training programme involved during a workout. This training gets you into top physical shape, firming and toning your body, reducing body fat and increasing both endurance and stamina. While burning calories and working up a sweat, kickboxers are simultaneously learning to fight and defend themselves. The confidence gained by kickboxing is another aspect which appeals to both men and women. Kickboxing for the purposes of health, fitness and self-defence has become one of the biggest trends in the fitness industry since aerobics.

Women in kickboxing

More and more women worldwide are flocking to kickboxing classes. Most of them see the training as a most effective and practical means of learning to defend themselves should they need to do so while, at the same time, getting physically fit and mentally tough. Women (who are usually more practical than men) find that kickboxing provides an attractive and stimulating alternative to the sometimes monotonous training methods used in traditional martial arts. Combining full-contact fighting systems with boxing techniques in an intense workout burns up calories and provides a fantastic cardiovascular training session. Women also love kickboxing training because it helps to burn up fat, tones and firms the body, and stimulates the mind and develops a strong positive mental attitude.

Nowadays, they also compete internationally at the highest levels. Christine Banner and Kathy Long from the USA are world champions and respected kickboxers who have attained something akin to superstar status.

above FEMALE KICKBOXERS WORKING OUT. IN THE FOREGROUND IS AN EXAMPLE OF A ROUNDHOUSE KICK ON THE HEAVY BAG. BAG WORK IS VITAL TO DEVELOP YOUR PUNCHES AND KICKS FOR FIGHTING COMBINATIONS. THE WOMAN IN THE BACKGROUND IS SHADOW SPARRING AGAINST AN INVISIBLE OPPONENT. SKIPPING (NOTE ROPE ON THE FLOOR) FORMS A VITAL PART OF THE TRAINING ROUTINE.

TECHNICAL ELEMENTS

Modern kickboxing was born out of a desire to establish a martial art that would be effective in close-combat fighting, either in the street or as a full-contact, stand-up fighting sport.

By the late 1960s, traditional martial artists in the USA discovered to their dismay that their techniques did not work in combat situations. They realized the need to develop a full-contact fighting system in order to be effective in combat. As they were pulling back on their punches and kicks, instead of driving them in with impact and force, their techniques were proving ineffective. Furthermore, traditional karate techniques are practised in a predetermined pattern that looks fine in a dojo (training studio) but does not work in combat; would-be assailants do not follow rites, rituals or predetermined patterns when trying to assault you.

To add insult to injury, the traditionalists soon discovered that their fitness and conditioning was not geared to withstanding full-contact punches and kicks to the head or body. They could barely endure one round of full-contact sparring. Out of these and many other perceived shortcomings in some of the traditional martial arts, modern-day kickboxing was born.

Pioneer kickboxers in the USA turned to the training, conditioning and fighting techniques of western professional boxing in the early seventies. From them they learnt more appropriate training, conditioning and fighting strategies of full-contact fighting and absorbed them into their fledgling sport, along with boxing's rules and regulations. Over several years, and as a result of fighting in full-contact bouts, kickboxers began to discover, through actual experience, which techniques and combinations were effective in a combat situation and which were not.

More and more, they began to train as professional boxers would, doing roadwork (running), skipping, heavy punch bag work, focus and Thai-pad work as well as medicine ball training. With determination they would spar for virtually hundreds of rounds in preparation for bouts, training their bodies and minds as they toughened and conditioned themselves by absorbing endless punches and kicks. Like boxers, they also wore protective equipment during sparring to protect themselves from injury. As the sport and combat fighting art of kickboxing grew, kickboxers improved tremendously, their techniques became strong and powerful and they were fitter, better conditioned and mentally tougher. Kickboxing bouts also became more action-packed and exciting.

Because kickboxing is a combat martial art it is important to take precautions to protect yourself during training. When training for fitness and self-defence, or when preparing for an upcoming fight, you must always wear protective safety equipment while sparring. Equipment to be worn includes head guards, gum guards, shin guards, kick boots and groin guards. Great care must be taken to bandage your hands correctly before bag punching, pad work and sparring. And always do your warm-up exercises and stretching properly before a workout.

The techniques shown in this chapter are not all allowed in the various kickboxing sport disciplines. Low kicks, for example, are only used in low kicks and Thai boxing, while knees, elbow strikes and throws are allowed only in Thai boxing. For semi-, light- and full-contact kickboxing the target area is strictly above the belt for all punches and kicks.

To master the basic techniques of kickboxing you must practise each technique many times before moving on to the next one. There is a saying in kickboxing that repetition is the mother of skill. So practise and persevere daily in your training.

opposite TWO FEMALE KICKBOXERS TRADE KICKS DURING A LIGHT-CONTACT KICKBOXING TOURNAMENT.

The basic techniques of kickboxing

Fighting stance

A kickboxer's fighting stance (A) is virtually the same as for boxing; feet about shoulderwidth apart, knees slightly bent, left glove held about eye level and right glove at cheek level. The distance between the fists and face should be about the width of a glove. Elbows should be resting lightly against the rib cage and pointing downwards. Finally, turn your body to the right and adopt a slight crouching pose.

This is the best stance for kickboxing as your weight is just forward enough for explosive punching and kicking. This stance also prevents you from being easily knocked down or off balance. You also have a balanced posture at all times from which you can attack, counter or defend without any preliminary movement.

A

Footwork

To practise your footwork, assume the fighting stance and keep your hands up at all times. To move towards your opponent, step forward with your left foot and then slide your right foot up and assume your normal stance position. Ensure that you are always totally relaxed and perfectly on balance. Continue shuffling forward for 10 steps.

To practise moving backwards, assume your fighting stance, step back with your right foot and then slide your left foot back to your fighting stance position. Continue to practise shuffling backwards for about 10 steps. Once you are comfortable shuffling forward or back you can practise these moves in a free form, taking two steps forward then two steps back, and so on.

Next comes the sidestep. To sidestep to the right, first step to your right with your right foot and then slide your left across towards your right foot so that your feet are in the normal fighting stance position.

For sidestepping to the left, first step to your left with your left foot, then slide your right foot across to the right, assuming your normal fighting stance. Bring all the individual steps together by combining your forward and backward footwork with sidestepping to the right and left in a free style form; shuffle forward, sidestep to the right, shuffle backward, sidestep to the left. Once you have mastered the footwork drills you will be able to launch your attacks, or defend and counterattack, automatically.

Range

There are three different classifications of 'range' in kickboxing, namely long, medium and close range. The range at which you find yourself during an actual bout determines the type of strategy and the techniques you should use in order to defeat or get the better of your opponent. If you are tall and have a longer reach than your opponent, you should throw left jabs and straight rights, as well as front kicks, to keep him well away and at the end of your punches and kicks, thus preventing him from getting too close to you.

↘ Long range

Long range (A) is used for explosive power punching and kicking. It is also the distance at which you can step in and fell your opponent with a straight punch or kick (B). You can also counter punch or kick from a long range when your opponent attacks you.

☜ Medium range

This is the range (A) where you can throw rapid-fire combinations of punches (B) and kicks without having to step forward. Medium range suits the aggressive kickboxer and fighter who likes to keep busy by pressurizing his opponent with a combination barrage of punches and kicks.

⇨ Close range

This range is for close-quarter combat where two opponents stand toe-to-toe and trade punches, like hooks (A) and uppercuts (B), as these are more effective at close range.

Punching
Boxing techniques — the jab

The first punch a kickboxer or boxer learns is the jab to the head. The jab is used to keep your opponent at bay and to score points at either long or medium range. Most good trainers tell their fighters to 'fight behind the jab' because, by so doing, not only do you score points and discourage your opponent from moving in, but you also set him up for a powerful right cross or kicks to the body.

⇨ **The jab to the head**
From your fighting stance position (A) step forward with your left leg and deliver a left jab to your opponent's head (B). When executing the left jab make sure that you put your body weight behind the punch and tuck your chin in. To develop a lightning-fast powerful jab you should practise throwing hundreds of left jabs against the punching bag and focus pads until it becomes an automatic reflex.

⇦ **Jab to the body**
When throwing a jab to the body it is important to put your entire weight on your left foot and then step forward and punch (a). If you do this your body jab will generate tremendous force and impact. When delivering this punch you should slip your body to the right in order to avoid a right counterattack from your opponent.

⇦ The right cross

From your fighting stance, step forward with your left foot and throw a straight right punch to your opponent's chin. When throwing the right cross, turn your right shoulder into the punch and place your body firmly behind it (A). You should never lead with the right cross — instead, first probe your opponent's defence with jabs and double jabs, which should create an opening for your right. The right cross is also used as a powerful counter punch.

⇨ Right to the body

When executing a right to the body you need to slip to your left, bend your knees and whirl your right shoulder as you punch (a). A right to the body is usually thrown after a jab to the head, following it up by delivering the powerful right to the body. Kickboxers today rarely concentrate on body punches, so practise the right to the body until it becomes automatic. A strong right to the solar plexus (delivered at the right time) is capable of stopping your opponent.

Hooks

The correctly executed hook is a powerful weapon. An outside hook must be landed with the elbow pointed out away from the body while whirling your shoulder and hips with the punch. Hooks must not be thrown from the long range otherwise they will degenerate into a swing. Hooks to the face or body must be thrown at medium to close range (A).

The left hook

From your fighting stance, execute the left hook to your opponent's head while rotating your shoulders, hips and left foot simultaneously as you drive your punch home (a). Make sure that, when you land your hook on target, you also twist your fist so that your thumb is pointing towards you. When you practise the hook make sure that you keep the elbow up and well away from your body. Properly done, the hook is an explosive, pure knockout punch that will not fail to produce results, especially when it targets the opponent's stomach area (b).

The right hook

The right hook is thrown the same way as the left hook, except that you rotate your right shoulder and hip into the punch as you explode your right fist on the side of your opponent's jaw or temple.

You should also practise throwing left hooks followed by right hook, whirling your shoulders from side to side with each punch.

Shovel hooks

Shovel hooks are thrown from your fighting stance and are used at close range in fighting. Executed correctly, the shovel hook is one of the most explosive short punches that you can throw at close quarters.

⇦ The shovel hook to the body

When delivering the left shovel to the body make sure that your elbow is against your body before you whirl your hips and entire body to your right as you explode the punch into your opponent's body (A). When landing on the target your fist should be at an angle of about 45 degrees, with your palm facing towards you.

The right shovel hook to the body is thrown exactly the same way as the left, except that you twist your hips and shoulders to the left as you execute the punch. When throwing a right shovel you must shift your body to your right, placing your weight on your right foot, before executing the punch.

⇧ Shovels to the head

Head shovels are thrown from your normal stance. Keep your left elbow against your rib cage, then rotate your hips and shoulders as you deliver the punch to your opponent's jaw (a).

The uppercut

An uppercut is a punch delivered from close range which travels straight up inside your opponent's guard. Before throwing an uppercut your knees must be bent and, as you punch, straighten your knees to generate an upward surge with your whole body. This will create tremendous impact when the uppercut lands on target.

⇨ The left uppercut

From close range, in your fighting stance, bend your knees and, as you deliver the left uppercut between your opponent's guard, surge your hips and shoulders in an upward movement as you hit your opponent, either on his jaw or to his solar plexus.

The right uppercut

The right uppercut is more powerful than the left as you can generate a greater upward surge with your knees, hips and shoulders as you deliver the punch (A). It can also be effective — using a short step — to straighten up a crouching or bobbing fighter.

⤺ The back fist strike

The left back fist strike to the head is used as a lightning strike to blind your opponent and set him up for a powerful right punch or kick to the body. From your stance draw your left arm across your face, elbow slightly up (A), then execute a rapid back fist strike, landing with the knuckle part of the glove on your opponent's head (B). The best way to set up a back fist strike is to first jab your opponent's body.

⤵ The spinning back fist strike

The spinning back fist is a surprise attack and, to be effective, must be executed in one movement without hesitation. The spinning back fist is best thrown after a jab to the body which turns your opponent's attention down, thus leaving his head exposed. To deliver the spinning back fist, first pivot on your left foot (a) before rotating your right foot and body 180 degrees clockwise (b). Finally, smash the back fist strike to your opponent's jaw or temple (c). Make sure that you turn your head to enable you to see your opponent. You must land your strike with the knuckle part of your glove — striking with your forearm or elbow is a foul.

Combination punching

It is important that you learn the correct combinations, both in boxing and kickboxing. The combinations taught to you by your trainer have been tried and tested in the ring or in actual street combat, so they work 100 per cent. Combination punching or kicking creates openings in your opponent's defence for you to land a knockdown or knockout strike .

↘ The left-right cross combination

This is the classic one-two or left-right cross combination that is thrown in rapid succession with maximum power. The object of this combination is to land that big right cross on your opponent. The left-right cross can either be used as an attack or as a counterattack as your opponent moves in. From your fighting stance, take a step forward and fire the left-right cross in a straight line into your opponent's face (A & B). Practise the left-right cross combination until it becomes second nature, as it is one of the most potent strikes in boxing or kickboxing.

The double jab and right cross

The double jab and right cross combination is thrown the same as the left-right cross, except that you double up on the left jab as you step in, thus paving the way for your right cross. The double left jab can be used as an effective combination or even on its own. It is a fantastic points-scoring strike. When executing the double jab make sure that your second jab is just as powerful as your first.

The left-right cross and left hook combination to the head

From your stance, step forward and throw a left-right to the head, followed by a powerful left hook to the side of the jaw or temple. The left hook is a deadly punch (one of the most lethal punches in kickboxing or boxing), and when thrown with maximum power in this combination can result in a knockdown or knockout. The main objective of this combination is to open up your opponent to a potent left hook to his head.

↘ Jab to the face, jab to the body, right cross to head

In this combination you are first striking to the head (A), then to the body (B), and finally to the head again (C). This combination should be executed in a smooth and rhythmic motion, with the emphasis being on delivering the last right cross punch with explosive impact. The objective of this combination is to hit your opponent with your powerful right to the head. When you throw the left jab to your opponent's body you should bend your legs and lower your body. This creates the impression in your opponent's mind that you are concentrating your attack on his body, but instead you straighten up your body and throw the right cross over his guard.

The left jab / left hook / right uppercut

Step in toward your opponent and throw a left jab (A), then a left hook (B), followed by a strong right uppercut between your opponent's guard (C). Throwing a left jab, followed by a left hook, is called 'hooking off the jab' and must be practised assiduously to perfect this double punch. This is a classic combination and is usually thrown from medium range. If the left hook does not damage your opponent the right will breach his defence by coming through his guard. Practise this combination repeatedly on the heavy bag and focus pads.

The right uppercut / left hook

This combination is delivered at close range and is extremely effective. Drive the right uppercut between your opponent's arms and follow it up with a left hook to his jaw. This combination can also be used when your opponent is on the ropes.

↘ The right cross / left shovel / left hook / right uppercut

This is an interesting combination as it creates openings in your opponent's defence. Throw the right cross to your opponent's jaw (A) and follow it up with a left shovel to his liver (B), a left hook to the head (C) and finally a stiff right uppercut (D).

Defence against punches

Defence includes preventing your opponent's punch from landing as well as how you can counter with your own punch. You must be able to prevent punches thrown to your head or body from landing. You can do this by evading the punch by slipping, bobbing and weaving, pulling away or side-stepping, or else by blocking the punch with your hand, forearm, elbow or shoulder. Developing a good defence against punches is of primary importance as it prevents you from being hit too many times during a bout.

⇨ **Blocking the left jab**

For blocking straight punches, the left jab should be blocked by your right hand. Take your stance in front of your sparring partner and let him throw a slow left jab to your face; block this jab with your open right palm (A). Keep your eyes open at all times when you are practising blocking, as well as during sparring.

After you have practised blocking your sparring partner's left jab many times, start to counter with your own left jab to his face (B).

Make sure that when you block your opponent's left jab you are on balance and that you parry the punch just enough to miss your head.

⇨ **Blocking the straight right**

When your sparring partner throws a lead straight right to you from a normal stance, block his right fist with your left hand and throw your own right to his jaw. If you find yourself out of position, and that you have dropped your left arm, you must block the straight right lead with your left shoulder. Hunch your left shoulder up and whirl to your right, tucking your chin behind the shoulder. Your opponent's right punch will then land on your shoulder.

⇨ Blocking straight punches to the body

To block a straight jab to your body, turn to the left and block the punch with your right forearm or your elbow (a). To block a straight right to your body, turn to your right and block the punch with your left elbow (A).

⇨ Blocking a left and right hook to the head

A left hook to the head must be blocked with your right forearm (b). You can then counter the left hook with a left uppercut to your opponent's chin. A right hook to the head must be blocked with your left forearm (B). Counter with your own right shovel or uppercut.

⇨ Blocking a right uppercut

You can block your opponent's right uppercut to the head or body by dropping your forearm or hand on to his upcoming fist or forearm (C). You can then counter with your own left hook to the side of the head.

⇨ **Deflecting or parrying**

Deflecting or parrying is used against straight punches to the head or body. As your sparring partner throws a left jab to your head you deflect his punch with your open right hand. His jab will pass over your left shoulder (A). The parry is done without effort and does not affect your balance. The parry spins your opponent off balance and leaves him open to be countered with a left shovel to the body.

↘ **Parrying a straight right to the head**

As your opponent throws a straight right to your head you parry his wrist with your opened left hand (a). You can now counter with your own right punch to his body.

Evasion

Evasion is a defensive move whereby you make your opponent miss a punch without any contact being made. It is the best method of defence because it throws your opponent off balance and thus opens him up for your counterattack. Evasion is achieved by slipping, bobbing and weaving, using footwork or by dropping away. The best form of evasion is to not make contact with your opponent as this throws him off balance. This is achieved by slipping, bobbing and weaving or side-stepping.

⇦ **Slipping the left jab to the head**

Let your sparring partner throw a slow motion left jab to your head. As the punch comes, slip it to your right by rolling your left shoulder forward and down. The jab will pass over your left shoulder (A). Practise slipping the left jab about 30 times to become accustomed to the movements, after which you will be ready to counter the jab. When your sparring partner throws the jab, artfully and quickly slip it and step in with your own left to the body.

Slipping a right cross to the head

As your sparring partner throws a right to your head, slip his punch to your left by rolling your right shoulder forward and down. His right will pass over your right shoulder. After enough practice you will get used to slipping the right cross, at which point you can start to counter with your own right smash to the body.

⇦ **The bob and weave**

The aim of the bob and weave is to create a moving target of your head and make your opponent uncertain of which way you will slip if he punches you (A). The bob and weave must always be executed with a relaxed, flowing movement in order to be effective.

The bob and weave to a left hook to the head

As your sparring partner throws a left hook to your head, bob down quickly and weave to your right (a). As the punch passes straight past your head you can come up and counter with a straight right to his jaw (b).

The bob and weave to a right hook to the head

When your opponent throws a right hook to your head, bob down and weave to your left, come up and throw your own left hook to the side of his head (as for the left hook).

⇨ **The pull away**

As your sparring partner throws a left jab you sway backwards, shifting your weight onto your right foot (A). His jab will fall short and you will be able to counter with your own jab or right cross as you bring your weight forward. Some kickboxers drop their hands (and their guard) to effect a full-swing body movement backwards.

Kicking techniques

Kicks are three or four times more powerful than punches, especially when thrown to your opponent's body. Always kick with maximum power, putting your hips behind the kick. In an actual full-contact bout, weak and ineffective kicks do not score points. Always follow up your kicks with punches or, when punching first, follow up with your kicks. When delivering any kick, you should do so in one fast, fluid motion.

⇨ **The front kick**

The front kick delivered off your front leg is executed in the same way as the left jab in boxing. You can stop your opponent with a strong left front kick to his midsection when he moves in to attack you, or you can use the front kick as a mid- or long-range attack. From your onguard position, lift your knee and point to your opponent's midsection (A) and then execute a strong front kick (B). To develop power kicks you must practise for hours against the punch bag. The ball of the foot is used as the striking surface. Beginners might be inclined to keep their toes straight — this will lead to injury.

⇦ **The rear leg front kick**

The front kick executed with the back leg is more powerful than the front kick with the lead leg because you can get more power by utilizing your hips and body as you drive the kick into your opponent. You use your front kick with your lead leg the same way as you would a left jab. You can keep your opponent at bay or stop him as he comes in for an attack, thereby opening him up to other counterattacks.

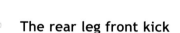

The roundhouse kick

The roundhouse kick is used more than any other kick in kickboxing. It is delivered with the instep or lower shin with full powered impact into the body or head. Explosive power is generated by pivoting your supporting foot and rotating your hips and body into the roundhouse kick.

⇨ **Front roundhouse kick**

To throw the left roundhouse kick to the body or head, lift your left leg about 45 degrees and point your knee to the area of your opponent where you would like to land the kick (A). Then pivot on your right foot and rotate your hips as you deliver the kick (B).

⇩ **Rear roundhouse kick**

As you throw the right roundhouse kick, lift your right leg 45 degrees, point your knee to the target area (a), pivot on your left foot and rotate your hips with the kick as you execute it to the body or the head of your opponent (b).

⇩ The side thrust kick

Slide left leg up, raise your right leg and cock your knee (A), then kick on a straight line into your opponent's body, making contact with the heel of your foot (B). It is important that you lean your body backward as you execute this kick. The side thrust kick can be used as an attacking or a defensive kick. The side thrust kick is one of the most powerful kicks in kickboxing and must be practised daily on the heavy bag, as indeed should all your other kicks. The critical component of this kick is a powerful twist of your hips which drives the heel of the kicking foot into your opponent's body. Otherwise the 'kick' is simply a push.

⇩ The spinning back kick

For the spinning back kick to be effective it must be executed in one movement and with lightning speed. (It is demonstrated here in three stages.) From your fighting stance (A), pivot on your front foot and slide your right foot to your right side, so that your back is turned to your opponent (B). Look at him over your right shoulder, then bring your right knee up and shoot the back kick out into his mid-body region (C). When delivering a spinning back kick you must do it in one fast movement.

⇧ The hook kick

The hook kick, or reverse roundhouse, is very deceptive as it comes around your opponent's guard. To execute the front hook kick, slide your back foot up in one movement, taking the place of your front foot, then raise your left leg bringing your knee towards your body (A). Pivot on your right foot and lean your body back as you throw the hook kick from the outside in and around your opponent's guard (B).

⇧ The axe kick

The axe kick comes from above and down onto your target, which is your opponent's head, face or upper shoulders. Its name is derived from the downward chopping motion. The axe kick is quite easy to avoid, so it must be executed with perfect timing and at the right moment, ideally when your opponent is dazed or off balance. For the front left axe kick, swing your left leg outside and to the left of your opponent's body (A) in a circular motion to above head height. Smash your kick down on him, landing with your heel (B).

↘ The spinning back hook kick

To throw the spinning back hook kick from medium range in your stance position (a), pivot on your front foot as you whirl your body around 180 degrees (b) and swing your right leg in an arc, aiming the kick at your opponent's head (c). This kick generates tremendous power and, if it lands properly on target, usually results in a knockdown or KO. This kick is generally thrown after a punching combination attack to your opponent's head, or else when your opponent has dropped his guard.

⇓ The jumping front kick

The jumping front kick is used as a surprise attack and is aimed at your opponent's face. From your fighting stance, jump up and tuck your knees in close to your chest (A), before shooting out the left front jump kick to your opponent's face (B).

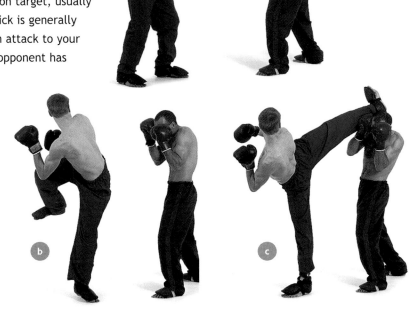

⇨ The jumping side kick

The jumping side kick is used if you have stunned your opponent with a punch or kick, or if he is retreating. Even if this kick is blocked, the force will drive your opponent back, opening him up to further attacks. From your fighting stance, jump up and forward, bringing your right leg up close to your chest and shoot out the side kick to your opponent's body (A).

Low kicks

Low kicks are allowed in kickboxing contests and in Thai boxing. Low kicks are not allowed in full-contact bouts, which consist of kicking and punching above the waist only. The low kick can have devastating effects and is the cause of many knockouts.

⇨ The outside low kick

This kick is thrown at the outside of your opponent's left thigh and is delivered with the lower shin or instep. The technique is the same as for the round-house kick, except that it is thrown to your opponent's legs. From your fighting stance, pivot on your front foot and rotate your hips and body as you drive the low kick into your opponent's outer thigh (a).

⇦ The low inside kick

Pivot on your right foot and drive the low kick into your opponent's inside thigh (A). Low kicks are thrown after a punching attack to your opponent's head as this paves the way to kick his legs with an inside or outside low kick. When you low kick your opponent, always keep your guard up as your opponent might counter your low kick with a right cross or stiff left jab.

Knee kicks

Knee strikes are allowed in Thai boxing and are a most effective technique. The knee is a potent weapon in close combat self-defence and can be used to attack either the groin, side ribs, solar plexus or face. Always arch your lower back and thrust your hips forward to ensure maximum impact.

⇦ The front knee kick

To execute the front knee kick, grasp your opponent firmly with both hands behind the head and pull him down onto your knee, striking him either to the head or midriff. You can bombard your opponent with left and right front knee kicks. Maintain an upright stance and don't allow your opponent to pull your head down.

⇩ The side knee kick

Hold your opponent's head, lift your right leg sideways (A) and smash your knee into his body (B). In this clinch position you can strike to his ribcage with both your knees in an effective combination. Whenever you are close up to your opponent you can grab him and deliver knee kicks.

⇦ The jumping knee kick

This is a surprise attack and must be executed in one fast movement. As you jump in and upwards at your opponent, grasp his head and pull it down with your arms as you knee him to the head. This technique is launched whenever you are in range and, because it is a surprise attack, it must be executed without any hesitation.

Elbow strikes

Elbow strikes are used in Muay Thai or Thai Boxing and are an extremely dangerous weapon due to the fact that the elbow is, of course, one of the hardest parts of the body. For close combat fighting and self-defence, the elbow is a deadly weapon, just like the knee. Elbow strikes are executed at medium or close range. Make sure that you rotate your hips and shoulders with all your elbow strikes in order to ensure maximum impact.

⇨ **The front elbow strike**

The front elbow strike is delivered like a hook punch but, instead of your fist hitting the target, you whip your elbow around and in to your opponent for a powerful blow to the head. You can use front elbow strikes against your opponent as an attack or as a counterattack after you have blocked a left or right punch to your head or body. You can also follow a left or right straight punch to your opponent's head with a front elbow strike delivered with the same arm.

⇦ **The downward elbow strike**

The downward elbow strike is used when your opponent comes in low, boring in at you with his head. It can also be used to strike the top of your opponent's head. To execute this technique, jump up close in to him and then, as you come down, smash your elbow on top of his head. You can also use the downward elbow strike when you pull your opponent's head down after grabbing him around the neck. Practise caution when employing this technique during sparring.

⇨ **Upward elbow strike**

From a fighting stance, throw your left upward elbow strike between your opponent's guard to strike him in the face. To deliver the upward elbow strike you have to get inside your opponent's guard at close range. You need to get one of your arms inside and between your opponent's guard to enable you to execute the upward elbow strike.

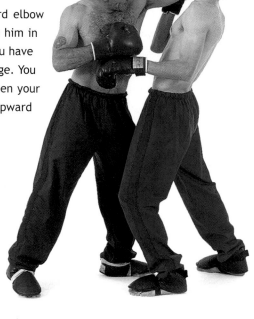

⇦ **Side elbow strike**

Step in from your fighting stance and strike your opponent with a side elbow strike. As the picture shows, the side elbow strike is usually executed when you slip a straight punch to your head.

⇨ **Spinning back elbow strike**

Usually delivered after a left-right punch combination. Pivot around 180 degrees and strike your opponent with a spinning back elbow strike. As this technique is thrown as a surprise attack, your distance and twisting must therefore be perfect in order for it to succeed. This is an exceptionally effective technique for self-defence in street combat.

Sweeping

Sweeping your opponent's leg causes him to lose balance, thus enabling you to follow up with punches or kicks. A clean sweep can also result in your opponent being thrown to the floor.

⇨ **Outside foot sweep**

From your fighting stance, feint a left to your opponent's face and then sweep his foot with the sole of your foot; this should cause him to lose his balance.

⇩ **Inside foot sweep**

The inside foot sweep is executed in the same manner as the outside foot sweep, except that you sweep inside your opponent's left leg. Follow the inside sweep with a right to the jaw.

⇨ **Spinning back sweep**

Feint a left jab to your opponent's head, spin around 180 degrees, bend low, and sweep the inside of your opponent's leg with the lower part of your right leg. Follow up with a right back fist to his head.

Punching and kicking combinations

The secret to success in a kickboxing bout, or in actual street combat, is to use the correct fighting combinations. The golden rule of combinations is that, after landing a punch, you should follow up with a kick. If you attack with a kick, it is best to follow up with punches. These combinations should be practised on the heavy bag.

Combination 1

Left front kick and left-right punch to the head. Slide in and deliver a strong front kick to your opponent's body (A). Follow it up immediately with a left-right punch combination to the head (B & C). This is a basic combination attack. By attacking his body with a front kick you draw your opponent's guard down, paving the way for your left-right combination punch to his head.

Combination 2

Left-right punch to the face (A & B), followed by a strong roundhouse kick to his body (C). The object of every kick-boxing combination technique is to create openings in your opponent's defence which you can exploit to land effective punches or kicks to his body or head. If his defence is good it is usually the last technique of the combination thrown that actually lands. It is important that you throw *every* technique of any combination with maximum power. All combinations should be practised as drills during sparring as well as when doing bagwork.

Combination 3

Side thrust kick to the body (A), followed by a spinning hook kick to the head (B). This combination is used after you have feinted a straight left or right to your opponent's head. The object of the feint to the head is to bring your opponent's guard up high. This will allow you to execute the side thrust kick to his midsection, after which you can attack his head with a spinning hook kick.

The combinations in kick-boxing are infinite and your trainer will teach you many variations, depending on your individual style, strength, weaknesses and skills as a fighter.

Combination 4

Left jab to the head (A), followed by a spinning back kick to the body (B), a right back fist (C) and, finally, a left punch to your opponent's head (D). You need to execute this combination in one fluid, continuous movement. Think of all four techniques as one. Practise this repeatedly until it becomes automatic.

TRAINING & SPARRING

Kickboxing, like any sport, requires dedication and commitment. Since this sport incorporates potentially dangerous techniques, regular, concentrated training is essential to gain control over the movements and use them with precision and self-confidence at the correct time, without causing lasting damage to a sparring partner or opponent.

Expertise does not come from watching others, or reading about how kicks and punches should be executed, although this, too, is helpful. Only active training and sparring, either with an invisible opponent or a real one, will let you practise the techniques you have learned and teach you how to attack and counterattack in an actual situation and under pressure. Sparring will let you evaluate your own strengths, and counteract your weaknesses by concentrating your training on various aspects that may need improvement. Similarly, you will learn to sum up your opponent's strengths and weaknesses. You will learn to evade strong movements and use weaker ones to your advantage.

The benefits of kickboxing are numerous and so are its challenges and rewards, but they will only pay off with regular training. A few lessons taken at intervals will not get you into the top physical condition you desire, nor firm and tone your body.

The training programme outlined in this chapter must be followed six days a week when preparing for a kickboxing fight. If you are training for grading, physical fitness, conditioning, self-defence or to improve your skills, you should follow the training schedule three times a week.

Always begin your workout with warm-up exercises and stretching to prevent the possibility of pulling a muscle or injuring yourself. By the time you begin your skipping routine you will be completely warmed up. Skipping helps you to develop a spring in your legs and improves your footwork when engaging in an actual bout. Shadow sparring or boxing is, aside from actual sparring, the best training for conditioning and sharpening your reflexes.

Bag work develops all the muscles you will use in punching and kicking, enabling you to become an explosive, powerful puncher and kicker. Focus pad work develops your speed, power and timing and should never be neglected. Thai pads are essential, especially for Thai boxers, for practising low and high kicks, as well as knee and elbow strikes. Speed bag and floor-to-ceiling training improves your timing, speed and eyesight.

Sparring remains the most important training aspect to condition your body and mind for full-contact fighting. It is best to end your session with power exercises to strengthen and harden your muscles and to add power to your kickboxing techniques.

It is also important that you eat properly. You must ensure that you get the right nutrients for health, fitness and to prevent illness. Eat only natural, wholesome food and drink enough fresh fruit and vegetable juices. Take vitamin and mineral supplements.

You must have, and rigorously adhere to, a scientific training programme. It is also important that, at all times, you have a positive mental attitude and that you train with focused attention in all you do.

Aside from your usual formal and organized training under your personal instructor, you need to do your own training at home on a daily basis. Work on one aspect of kickboxing every day (for example, your kicks) which will allow you to perfect your technique with a concentrated and focused mind, rather than trying to cover too much at one time.

opposite THE THAI BOXER ON THE RIGHT HAS TRAPPED HIS OPPONENT AGAINST THE ROPES AND IS ABOUT TO COMPLETE A KNEE STRIKE TO HIS BODY.
above A LOW KICK COUNTERED BY A BLOCK WITH THE FRONT LEG.

Your kickboxing workout and training routine
Warm-up exercises and stretching

Always warm-up properly before commencing your full workout, and that includes stretching exercises for flexibility.

⇦ ### Exercise 1: Running from standing position

Lift your knees up and pump your arms as you run on the spot. Running on the spot can be done at a slow, medium or fast pace. It develops spring in your legs and is a great cardiovascular exercise.

⇨ ⇲ ### Exercise 2: Side jump

From the feet together position, jump and extend your legs sideways, landing with your feet wide apart. Then jump back to your starting position. Repeat several times.

⇩ ### Exercise 3: Knee jump strikes

As you bounce up and down, bring one knee up to your chest, at the same time, pull your hands down level with your raised knee. Keep repeating from side to side, left knee up, then right knee up, and so on.

Do 10—20 repetitions for these exercises

48

⇨ Exercise 4: Arm circles

Swing both arms forward in a full, complete circle for 15 repetitions, and then backwards for 15 repetitions. This exercise warms up your shoulders, arms and upper back muscles. Again, it can be done at a slow, medium or fast pace.

⇦ Exercise 5: Side bends

Stretch slowly to the right, hold, and then stretch to the left, keeping your hands in an arc above your head and shoulders as you move from side to side. Side bend stretches warm up and stretch all the muscles on the side of your body. Keep your legs straight when doing the side stretch — this will ensure that you derive the maximum benefits from the exercise. With each repetition you should strive to stretch lower down on your thigh.

⇨ Exercise 6: Backward and forward stretches

Stretch backwards and hold for the count of three, and then stretch forwards and touch the ground, again for the count of three. It is important to support your lower back during the backward stretches.

Do 10–20 repetitions for these exercises

⇨ **Exercise 7: Side twists**

Twist your trunk to the left and then to the right, with your arms held up and in front of your chest. This exercise warms up and tones your abdominal muscles. The side twist uses the same twisting of your body as when throwing hook or shovel punches. Make sure that you pivot on the ball of your right foot, and vice versa, which will ensure a fluid, twisting motion. This is the same technique you will employ when throwing hooks during sparring.

⇦ **Exercise 8: Jumping squats**

From a standing position, squat down, keeping your back straight, and then jump up off the ground, straightening the legs. This exercise strengthens and develops the legs, particularly the thighs. You can start with about 10 repetitions and gradually increase your jumping squats up to 50 repetitions. As jumping squats strengthen your leg muscles your kicks will become more powerful.

Do 10—20 repetitions for these exercises

⇨ **Exercise 9: Sit-ups**

Lie flat on your back on the ground and, as you sit-up, bring your knees up simultaneously. All variations of the sit-up are aimed at conditioning, toning and developing your abdominal muscles. The tempering of your midsection is vital for a kickboxer — one strong punch or kick to the stomach can knock out your wind, possibly causing you to lose your fight. In a street encounter, being winded will place you at the mercy of your attacker or attackers.

⇩ **Exercise 10: Push-ups**

From the basic push-up position, bend your arms until your chest touches the ground, then straighten your arms to complete the push-up. Use your fists as shown, but only when you have built up sufficient strength and confidence. Women may not have enough upper-body strength to perform these push-ups where weight is supported only by the toes and fists, and may lower their knees to the ground instead.

Do 10–20 repetitions for these exercises

Stretching routine

⇨ **Straddle stance stretches**

From a straddle stance, stretch as low as you can by 'bouncing' very slowly and gently. Every time you deepen your stretch in this way it will ease your muscles, allowing you to stretch down further. This is an advanced warm up — not for beginners.

⇩ **Front leg stretch**

Bend your right leg and stretch your left leg out, with your toes pointing upwards. Stretch your muscles by bouncing your hips up and down.

⇨ **Leg stretch swings**

From the standing position, swing your right leg straight forward and then to the side (A). Make sure that you keep your leg straight for a maximum stretch. Repeat with the left leg (B).

Do 10—20 repetitions for these exercises

At this stage you should be warmed-up and ready to begin your full kickboxing workout.

Your kickboxing workout and training routine

⇦ **Skipping**

Skipping develops your co-ordination, stamina and leg spring. Begin a workout by skipping for 15–20 minutes. Learn to skip by moving your foot forward and then backward as you skip. Also, bring the rope round twice for every one jump in the air. Once you have become proficient in skipping you will have a lot of fun improvising as you go along.

⇨ **Shadow sparring**

Shadow sparring or shadow boxing is, after actual sparring itself, the best exercise for conditioning your body and sharpening your technique. During shadow sparring you must imagine that you are fighting an actual opponent. As you shadow spar you must go through all the offensive and defensive movements at top speed.

Bag work

Punching and kicking the heavy bag is of prime importance as it develops all the muscles you need to become an explosive and powerful puncher and kicker. In all your training sessions you should do five to six rounds on the heavy bag.

You should then do three rounds on the focus pads, three rounds on the Thai pads, two rounds on the speed ball and two rounds on the floor-to-ceiling ball. Each round on the above equipment should be three minutes in duration. Take one minute to rest between each round.

If you are a beginner you should practise only one technique at a time on the bag until you have reached a more advanced level. For example, start with only throwing left jabs against the bag, then straight rights, then front kicks, and then move on to all of the other techniques. Once you have achieved a degree of proficiency you can start throwing combinations on the bag.

Speed bag training

Speed, or pear bag training improves your timing and speed. You should train on the speed bag by throwing a straight left, back hand left parry, or straight right, followed by a back hand right parry. You can also do the entire combination in a tattoo rhythm. This training develops your muscles and timing for punching from the whirl, as well as developing a powerful back hand block. You should practise your straight punches, hooks and shovels on the speed bag.

Floor-to-ceiling ball training

This piece of training equipment trains your eyes and sharpens your reflexes to a greater degree. Practise short 'rat-a-tat' punches with your left and right hands. You can also practise your hooks, shovels and uppercuts. At the same time as you practise these strikes you should also use the ball to practise slipping and weaving at random as it comes back to you after each punch. This training is also great for your distance and timing, which are important factors in sparring and fighting.

Focus pad work

Focus pad work develops your speed, power and timing to a higher degree. Your trainer takes you through the movements, calling the combinations he wants you to practise. Focus pad training must be practised at top speed and with full power. It is extremely hard work and demands total concentration. Practise your punching combinations, spinning back fist strikes, roundhouse kicks, hook kicks and front kicks on the focus pads, at all times concentrating on the perfect execution of these techniques. Your trainer will take you through drills which allow you to practise your bobbing and weaving while doing focus pad workouts.

Thai pad work

Thai pads bring added possibilities to your training. You can utilize the Thai pads to practise punching, kicking, knee and elbow strikes and various combination techniques. Your trainer can speed up the pace and intensify the work at his discretion.

Sparring — the most important training

Sparring is, by a long way, the most important apect for developing, conditioning and focusing your mind and body for fighting. There is no substitute for sparring, and you should spar at each training session, especially when training for an upcoming kickboxing bout.

Sparring not only improves your skill, it also tempers your body for fighting by forcing your muscles to become accustomed to the explosive, 'broken' rhythmic movements that distinguish kickboxing fighting from any other sport.

Due to the force with which the repetitive kickboxing movements are executed, kickboxing can be very tiring. In addition, in an actual bout, or when sparring in a gym, you are absorbing punches and kicks to the body and head, which tempers and conditions your body and develops muscles of steel.

Conditioning is important. The body must be able to withstand several fast sparring bouts. A kickboxer who has not had adequate sparring practise will be completely exhausted after only one or two minutes. Thus, sparring remains a primary means of training for anyone wishing to be successful.

If you are preparing for an amateur bout you should do four rounds of sparring every day leading up to the fight. If you are preparing for a professional title fight you should spar for at least eight to 10 rounds a day. Your trainer will time you, with each round of sparring lasting three minutes — allow one minute of rest between rounds.

ONLY THROUGH MANY YEARS OF TRAINING WILL YOU BE ABLE TO MATCH THE POWER AND PRECISION OF THE KICKBOXER ABOVE. HE HAS USED A FULL LEG EXTENSION TO EXECUTE A POWERFUL SPINNING BACK HOOK KICK.

End your workout with dynamic power exercises.

Dynamic power exercises

If you are just beginning to train for kickboxing you should try to do 10 repetitions of the power exercises shown. As you progress and develop, your trainer will increase the repetitions to 20 in some exercises and even 100 in others, like sit-ups. If you are an amateur or a professional kickboxer and your trainer is preparing you for an upcoming fight, he will intensify your power exercises by getting you to do about three sets of each extension, with as many repetitions as you can do. He will drive you to the stage where you can do no more due to total exhaustion.

⇨ **Exercise 1: Shoulder squats**

Take your partner onto your shoulders (A), as if you were lifting a champion in the air after his victory, and perform 30—50 squats (B) to strengthen your legs. Beginners should start gradually, never lifting more than their own body weight. When practising shoulder squats, it is important w to keep your back straight at all times to avoid injury. If you are a beginner you should start with just five to 10 squats. As you progress, you can increase the number until you can do 20 repetitions. You can then start doing more sets, for example, two sets of 20 and then three sets of 20 repetitions.

⇩ **Exercise 2 : Incline push-ups**

Let your partner hold you up by your ankles as you do 30—50 push-ups. Keep your back straight when practising push-ups and lower your body until your chest touches the ground (b), then straighten your arms as you push yourself up (a). Push-ups develop and strengthen the muscles in your arms, chest and shoulders, which is important to improve your punching power. Some kickboxers, especially those from a martial arts background, also do push-ups on their fists or fingers to strengthen the fists and hands.

⇦ **Exercise 3:**
Handstand push-ups

Do a handstand with your partner holding your knees for support and balance. Then perform about 10–20 handstand push-ups.

The handstand push-up is quite a difficult exercise to do as it requires you to push your entire body weight upward. If you are attempting this exercise for the first time you should let your training partner assist you by lifting your body up at the knees as you start your push-up. As you develop your arm and shoulder muscles, and increase your strength, you can then start doing the push-ups using your own strength. This exercise develops tremendous strength in your shoulders and arms and can be mastered through regular practise.

⇦ **Exercise 4: Sit-ups**

Lie on your back and hook your foot behind your partner's calves. He does the same. Then do 10–20 sit-up crunches together and in time with one another. You can vary this exercise by twisting your body to the left and right as you do the sit-up. This will condition and strengthen your side abdominal muscles as well.

Exercise 5: Leg stretches

As you execute a slow left side kick towards your training partner, he grabs your foot and your left hand, thereby supporting you so that you maintain your balance as he gently stretches your leg upwards. If you are not yet very flexible then your training partner should begin by stretching very slowly, and he should stop immediately on your command if you feel uncomfortable. This is important so that you do not injure a leg muscle.

Exercise 6: Forward bends

This exercise strengthens the lower back. Let your partner wrap his legs around your waist and fold his hands around your neck. Keeping your back and neck straight at all times, bend forward until your spine is almost parallel to the ground, then straighten up again. Repeat 20—30 times. You can start by doing the forward bend with your legs bent at the knee, until your back is strong enough to allow you to perform it with straight legs.

a

b

⇨ ⇘ **Exercise 7: Back neck bridge**

This exercise is for strengthening your neck. It is imperative for kickboxers to develop a powerful neck in order to absorb their opponent's punches and kicks to the head. Lie flat on your back, then lift your body off the ground as you rise onto the top of your head. Rock back and forth slowly, which will work your neck muscles with each movement.

To begin with you can start doing the neck bridge for five repetitions. If your neck is weak you can place both your hands on the floor to support your body weight, thereby making the exercise much easier for you. As you strengthen your weak muscles by daily practise you can work up to 50 repetitions. Always practise at a controlled pace when doing this neck exercise — never too fast. Place a pillow (not too wide) on the floor for your head to rest on, as doing this exercise on a hard surface is often painful on your head.

⇨ **Exercise 8 : Front neck bridge**

Lie on your stomach and slowly rise up onto the top of your head and rock back and forth. This neck exercise strengthens and develops your front neck muscles. Rock forward and backward on your head at a controlled pace. If you are not accustomed to this exercise, place both hands on the floor to support your body weight, which will make this exercise easier for you.

⇨ **Exercise 9: Leg stretch**
As your partner lies on his back and raises his leg, put your foot on his ankle and gently stretch the raised leg towards his head by using your hands to push it forward. You may also support your partner's kneecap to ensure that his leg is kept straight.

⇦ **Exercise 10: Side leg stretch**
As your partner lies on his side, grasp his foot with both hands and gently push and stretch his leg towards his head.

Roadwork

An absolute must for the kickboxer, running (referred to as roadwork by boxers), strengthens the legs and develops stamina. If you have to lose weight before a fight then wear warm, heavy clothes during your run. Mix up your running routine by suddenly sprinting, then jogging, then shadow sparring. Nearly all professional fighters prefer to do their roadwork early in the morning. Professional kickboxers do 8—16km (5—10 miles) of roadwork a day. Amateur kickboxers need to run some 5—8km (3—5 miles) miles a day.

THIS KICKBOXER IS WEARING THE CORRECT GEAR FOR ROADWORK. IT IS VITAL TO PAY PARTICULAR ATTENTION TO THE CORRECT CHOICE OF JOGGING FOOTWEAR. IN WINTER YOU SHOULD WEAR A TRACKSUIT, WITH A HOOD FOR YOUR HEAD, WHEN DOING ROADWORK. ALSO TRY TO DO YOUR ROADWORK IN A NATURAL AREA WHERE THERE IS MINIMUM AIR POLLUTION AND TRAFFIC.

Nutrition for the kickboxer

In order to enjoy optimum health and well-being and maintain top physical fitness, you must ensure that your body gets the correct nutrients. The most important are carbohydrates, proteins, fats, vitamins and water. These are readily digested and absorbed by the body and are necessary for energy, health and cellular growth.

In addition to proper nutrients and a regular diet, you must have plenty of fresh air and sunshine, as well as a regular exercise regime. You should only eat wholesome, natural foods like wheat, oats, soya products, nuts, raisins, dates, honey, fruit and vegetables. Dairy products like milk, yogurt and cheese are also beneficial, as is plenty of freshly squeezed fruit juice.

Sprout your own alfalfa seeds, soy beans, mung beans and fenugreek, to name a few. Alfalfa, in particular, contains all the known vitamins including K and B8, in addition to potassium, phosphorus, calcium and chlorophyll.

Just one half-cup of soy bean sprouts contains an amount of vitamin C equivalent to six glasses of orange juice. If you feed your body natural food you will be taking in all the vital enzymes, hormones, vitamins and minerals, beside the bulk of proteins, fats and starches, for ultimate nourishment and nutrition.

For kickboxers, or any other sportsperson for that matter, ensuring that you eat the right foods must be a top priority. Only if you follow a careful natural diet plan will your body be able to generate the energy and vitality that is needed to train hard every day.

Avoid fried and fatty meals at all cost, and do stay away from junk food, processed food, sweets and carbonated drinks as they will not do your body any good.

Read the labels and do not buy foods that contain additives, pesticides, preservatives and other chemicals. These harmful substances will hinder your body's progress toward a naturally healthy state.

Lastly, beware of meat and poultry which may have been contaminated with antibiotics or growth hormones. All are detrimental to your health and fitness.

Health and vitamin supplements

Apart from adhering to a well-balanced natural diet, you should also take health and vitamin supplements. You can never be 100 per cent sure that you are getting all the daily nutrients your body requires. Soil depletion, cooking, preservatives and pesticides destroy many nutrients that could be beneficial to our bodies.

Super-health products you should consider taking are spirulina, kelp, wheat, barley grass and ginseng. And, of course, a daily supplement of Vitamin C, Vitamin E, Vitamin B12, as well as multiple vitamins with chelated minerals is important.

Positive mental attitude

Cultivating a positive mental attitude is even more important than correct physical training and diet. 'Just as your body becomes that which you eat, so your mind becomes that which you think' is a yoga mantra from India. Thoughts are vibrations of energy and they affect the body right down to its cellular level.

'As you think, so you are,' said James Allen in *As A Man Thinketh*. Control your mind and your senses by only thinking positive thoughts and by focusing your mind on the goals that you want to achieve. Do not dwell on negative thoughts or emotions, for they will produce negative effects in your life. Focus only on the positive results you would like to achieve.

What you focus on mentally actually becomes your reality in life over time. You should consciously focus on the positive goals that you wish to achieve in kickboxing by using your imagination. Visualize the outcomes you are hoping to achieve — imagination has, after all, been described by the ancient masters as being 'the eye of the soul'.

Your focused attention is the energy and vital force that, when strongly held in your mind, will begin to attract the right people, conditions and circumstances to you, thus enabling you to achieve your goals in life, be they in kickboxing, business or your personal life.

How to train and focus your mind: visualization and concentration

To achieve your goals in kickboxing you must direct your thoughts with concentrated attention towards the object of your desire. Visualize the goals you wish to attain and hold these thoughts strongly in your mind. If you persist in this practise every day and continue to train regularly and with determination then, sooner or later, your goals will begin to materialize in the physical world.

Strengthen your attention and the visualization of your goals with daily affirmations. 'Every day, in every way, I'm getting better and better', sang John Lennon in his song *Beautiful Boy*. This saying has been used by countless mind power specialists, for anything from improving your skills and personal powers to healing the body of illness and disease.

Your subconscious mind will begin to accept these affirmations as being true – this will hasten the process of the manifestation of your affirmations. What you focus on in your mind will, over a period of time, eventually become your reality.

Zen and the martial arts warrior

Zen appeals to the warrior spirit because it is the direct way of reaching the truth. The truth cannot be attained by intellect or reason, it has to be intuitively perceived within one's innermost being.

The Buddha said that 'the summit of reality lies within you'. Zen discipline teaches the samurai warrior always to be single-minded and have one objective in mind; to fight with an empty mind, looking neither backward nor sideways, but moving forward to crush the enemy. To accomplish this, the fighter has to train himself with assiduity every day, through endless repetitions of the fighting techniques and sequences he has learned, until he becomes one with the technique.

Through perfect concentration of mind he thus empties his mind of all thoughts and attains the state of super consciousness. This state of mind is called mushin, which means 'empty mind' or 'no thought'. When mushin is realized, the mind knows no obstructions, no inhibitions and is freed from the thoughts of life and death, pain and loss, victory or defeat. The warrior's mind then becomes like a mirror, reflecting the movements of his opponent instantly and without thought, thus making him invincible in combat.

Where the warrior has the slightest feeling or fear of death, or of attachment to life, the mind loses its fluidity. The fluidity is non hindrance. When the mind is devoid of all fear it is free from all forms of attachments and it is then master of itself, free from all hindrances, stoppages and inhibitions. It then follows its own course like water.

Spiritually speaking, this is a state of egolessness because the warrior now forgets all that he has learned, because he is the learning itself and there is now no separation of learner and learning.

In what has been said thus far we can readily see how closely the art of fighting with or without weapons approaches that of Zen. Both require us to come to the attainment of ultimate reality which is emptiness and when this state is realized the samurai warrior transcends all limitations of mind and matter and beholds that reality within.

(Originally published in Boxing World *magazine)*

SPORT
KICKBOXING

As do many other martial arts, kickboxing has various types of competitive disciplines to choose from, each with its own set of rules and regulations. The various competition modes are semi-contact, light-contact, full-contact, low kicks, Thai boxing and musical forms and weapons.

In semi-contact, points are awarded for clean punches and kicks that are landed on your opponent. The referee and judges must actually see the technique strike the target. Awarding points based on the sound of the strikes is not allowed. All techniques must be delivered with reasonable power. Any technique that simply touches your opponent will not be scored. If the referee sees what he considers to be a valid point he will command 'stop' and immediately signal the score, as will the two other judges. At least two judges must agree on a score's legitimacy for it to be awarded.

Points are awarded for the degree of difficulty of the technique as follows:

Punch or hard techniques — 1 point
Kicks to the body — 1 point
Kicks to the head — 2 points
Jumping kicks to the body — 2 points
Jumping kicks to the head — 3 points

Semi-contact bouts consist of two two-minute rounds, with a one-minute rest between rounds. Each fighter must wear a clean kickboxing uniform with a belt around his waist that reflects his grade. Compulsory safety equipment includes head guards, gloves, shin guards, mouth guards and kick boots.

Competition in light-contact kickboxing should be executed with well-controlled techniques and with equal emphasis placed on punching and kicking. Light-contact has been created as an intermediate stage between semi- and full-contact kickboxing.

Bouts are also two two-minute rounds, with a one-minute rest between rounds. The referee controls the fight but he does not judge — the fight is judged by three judges placed on three sides of the fighting area. The uniform and safety equipment for light-contact is the same as for semi-contact.

Full-contact kickboxing bouts are fought in a boxing ring. The target area for full-contact is the same as in boxing, and in full-contact you can use all the techniques of boxing and kickboxing. Jabs, hooks, uppercuts, front kicks, roundhouse kicks, hook kicks, side and back kicks are all employed, thus making full-contact kickboxing an exciting spectator sport.

Amateur bouts are made up of three rounds of two minutes each, with one minute between rounds. Professional bouts for world title fights last 12 rounds, and for national titles they go to 10 rounds. Preliminary bouts can be anywhere from four to six rounds.

The referee controls the fight, ensuring that all the rules are obeyed. He deducts points at his discretion for continued fouls. A fighter who does not obey the referee's orders and who violates regulations can receive a caution, a warning or be disqualified.

Three judges placed on different sides of the ring score kickboxing bouts. At the end of a bout the kickboxer who has obtained a majority decision, as scored by the three judges, is declared the winner on points. A kickboxing bout can also be won on a knockout (KO), or technical knockout (TKO), either when the referee stops the fight or when the towel is thrown in. A fight can also be won on a disqualification.

In full-contact, a fighter's uniform consists of a pair of long kickboxing pants; male boxers leave the upper

opposite TWO MUAY THAI FIGHTERS IN A VILLAGE SPARRING SESSION. A STRONG ROUNDHOUSE KICK ATTACK HAS BEEN BLOCKED, OPENING UP A LOW KICK OPPORTUNITY FOR THE DEFENDER.

body bare, while women wear vests. Head guards, gum shields, groin guards, shin guards and kickboxing boots are compulsory.

However, no head guards are worn in professional bouts and brain damage becomes a serious concern. It is essential that a fighter undergo a full medical inspection after having been knocked out. (For the same reason, children should always wear head guards when sparring or fighting.)

Light-contact techniques must at all times be controlled. Punches and kicks to the head should be executed in a light-contact manner. Punches and kicks to the body can be delivered a bit stronger and more focused, but they must still be controlled — they must not be full-contact blows.

In low kicks the same rules as for full-contact apply, with kicks to the outer and inner thighs also being allowed. A low kick fighter must wear Thai boxing shorts. Shin pads are not allowed.

Amateur Thai boxing bouts last for three rounds of three minutes, with the professionals going five rounds of three minutes. Thai boxing shorts are compulsory and no protective gear is allowed on the legs or feet. Gloves and gum shields are compulsory, however, and in amateur bouts head guards are added to the compulsory list. Knee and elbow strikes are allowed in pro fights, as are low kicks to the thighs. No elbow strikes are allowed in amateur bouts.

Musical forms choreograph karate and other martial art techniques to music. The judging criteria are synchronization, showmanship, degree of difficulty, basics and balance, strength and focus. In musical weapon forms, competitors must show perfect control of their weapon. They are judged by the same criteria as used in musical forms, with manipulation of the weapon also being taken into account.

Kickboxing is not merely a sport — the majority of students practise kickboxing as a contact fighting martial art. The art of kickboxing and its philosophy has been described as an attitude of mind to be developed and a way of life to be practised.

Competition — amateur kickboxing

The leading and largest kickboxing amateur body in the world is WAKO, the World Association of Kickboxing Organizations. WAKO has 89 affiliated countries across the five continents. The WAKO World Championships, held every two years, unite all the national teams from around the world to compete in what many call the 'Martial Arts Olympics'. Each country may only enter one competitor in each weight class — normally their national champion.

In the WAKO World Championships, martial artists from all styles (kickboxing, karate, taekwondo, kung fu, tai chi or free style) compete under the same kickboxing rules in semi-, light- or full-contact, low kicks, Thai boxing and musical forms. WAKO thus guarantees the best-possible kickboxing fights and its gold medalists are true world champions.

Professional kickboxing

Just like professional boxing there are various world kickboxing bodies that sanction professional kickboxing titles in the various weight categories. The most prestigious of these world bodies are WKA (World Kickboxing Association), WAKO-Pro, ISKA (International Sport Kickboxing Association), KICK (Karate International Council of Kickboxing) and K-1 from Japan.

Professional world kickboxing title bouts are held around the world, and in just about every country they fight for national and professional titles.

TWO FEMALE THAI BOXERS IN ACTION DURING A BOUT. THE FIGHTER ON THE RIGHT IS DELIVERING A ROUNDHOUSE KICK TO HER OPPONENT'S BODY.

Different kickboxing sport disciplines

Kickboxers can choose to compete in various kickboxing sport competitions; semi-, light- or full-contact, low kicks, Thai boxing, musical forms or weapons.

Semi-contact kickboxing

Points are awarded in semi-contact for clean punches and kicks landed on your opponent. The punch or kick must make contact. As soon as a point is scored, the referee will halt the fight and award the point to the fighter who scored or made contact first. The bout then continues. The kickboxer who has the most points at the end of two rounds is declared the winner. Semi-contact is a fast, exciting sport based on speed and timing, and it produces the most technically perfect fighter.

Equipment and dress code for semi-contact

In semi-contact kickboxing you must wear a kickboxing uniform. It consists of a pair of long pants and a V-neck top with long sleeves, with the fighter's belt rank worn around the waist. Fighters must also wear gloves, head guards, gum

The woman kickboxer shown in this photo is wearing the correct dress code as well as the correct safety equipment for semi- and light-contact kickboxing.

shields, groin protection, shin pads and foot protectors. Women fighters should wear breast protectors.

Light-contact or continuous fighting

Light-contact fighters fight for two rounds of two minutes. The fight is not stopped after every hit, both competitors throw non-stop combinations. The referee only stops the fight when clinching occurs. After each round the three judges score the fight on the '10 point must' system. The contact must be light and controlled. In the '10-point must' system the main criterion is this: if both fighters are judged to be equal after a round then the judges will score the round 10 to 10 (10 points each). If one fighter is landing more punches and kicks than his opponent then he will score 10 points to his opponent's nine points. If there is a knockdown in a particular round in full-contact or Thai boxing, then that round will be scored 10 to 8 in favour of the fighter who knocked his opponent down. There are no knockdowns in light-contact as it is against the rules.

Equipment and dress code for light-contact

In light-contact kickboxing bouts, both the uniform and the equipment is precisely the same as for semi-contact fights.

Full-contact

All full-contact kickboxing bouts are fought in a boxing ring. The target area in full-contact is the same as in boxing. All punches and kicks must be above the belt. Amateur bouts last for three rounds of two minutes. Professional kickboxing bouts can be from four to six rounds in preliminary bouts, up to 10 rounds for national titles, and 12 rounds for world title bouts, depending on which world sanctioning body is involved. Three judges score the fight on a '10 point must' system (*see page 70*). You can win either on points, by TKO (technical knockout) or by a straight knockout. Full-contact utilizes all the techniques of boxing and kickboxing. Jabs, hooks, uppercuts, front kicks, roundhouse kicks, hook kicks, side kicks and spinning back kicks are all employed, making full-contact exciting and spectacular.

The kickboxer pictured here is wearing the correct safety equipment for a full-contact bout — head guard, gum shield, gloves, groin guard, shin guards and kickboxing boots. In full-contact the fighter must wear long kickboxing pants — however, the kickboxer on the right is wearing Thai shorts in order to show the correct safety equipment.

The referee plays a vital role in full-contact bouts — he inspects the fighters to ensure that they are wearing the proper safety equipment and that they conform to the proper dress code. He also goes to each fighter's dressing-room before the bout to instruct them under which rules they will be fighting. He will also inspect their taped hands to make sure that the taping conforms to the rules. He must referee the fight strictly according to the rules, will give warnings to the fighters and, if necessary, deduct points for repeated fouls. He will also direct a fighter to a neutral corner after a knockdown and has the power to disqualify a fighter if necessary. He also does the 10-count in the event of a knock-down or knockout.

Equipment and dress code for full-contact

Fighters wear long kickboxing pants, gloves, gum shields, groin guards, shin pads and kickboxing boots. Women wear breast protectors. Head guards are compulsory in amateur kickboxing. Male kickboxers' upper torsos are bare in amateur and professional kickboxing.

Thai boxing

This differs from full-contact in that low kicks and knees to the body or head are allowed, as well as elbows and throws. As a result, this is the toughest of all kickboxing disciplines.

There is some confusion regarding the difference between Thai boxing and Muay Thai. The rules of Thai boxing as practised as a sport in the West differ from the rules of Muay Thai in Thailand insomuch as punching techniques carry the same weight as kicks and knee strikes and are scored accordingly. The use of elbows is also forbidden in Thai boxing.

In Muay Thai the ceremony called Wai Khru is compulsory before every bout. In addition, punches, no matter how valid or effective, are given little importance by the judges in Thailand. Low kicks, throw downs, knees and elbow techniques are given preference in terms of points. Furthermore, Muay Thai is deeply connected to its country of origin, Thailand, both spiritually and culturally. Muay Thai is, therefore, a difficult product to export, which explains why Thai boxing is both preferred and promoted in countries in the West.

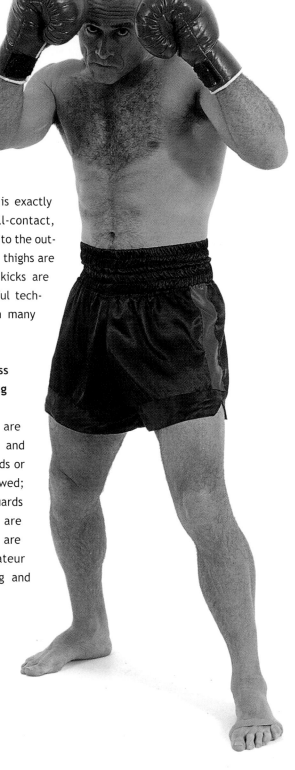

Low kicks

Low kick kickboxing is exactly the same as full-contact, except that low kicks to the outside and inside of the thighs are allowed. These low kicks are an extremely powerful technique that results in many knockouts.

Equipment and dress code for Thai boxing and low kicks

Thai boxing shorts are worn in Thai boxing and low kicks. No shin pads or kick boots are allowed; only gloves, mouth guards and groin guards are worn. Head guards are compulsory in amateur bouts in Thai boxing and low kicks.

The kickboxer seen in this photo is wearing the proper dress code for a Thai boxing bout. Gloves, gum shield, Thai shorts and a groin guard are only required for professional Thai boxing. Head guards are compulsory during an amateur bout.

THE THAI BOXER ON THE RIGHT LANDS A ROUNDHOUSE KICK TO HIS OPPONENT'S HEAD DURING A BOUT.

Musical forms and weapons

Musical forms are martial art techniques practised in a set sequence and choreographed to music of the competitor's choice. The techniques used by competitors are spectacular, aerodynamic and make for an entertaining spectator sport. Musical forms are included as a separate sport competition by kickboxing organizations who also do semi- and light-contact.

The martial artists who compete in musical forms are judged in a similar manner to gymnasts. They are awarded points ranging from 9.5 to 10. The winner is the fighter with the most points in total awarded by the five judges.

Equipment and dress code for musical forms and weapons

Musical weapon forms are judged largely on the mastery of the chosen weapon, for instance short range weapons like knives, clubs, sai, tonfa or the kama. Otherwise, they are scored on the same system as musical empty-hand (karate) forms.

Grading

Like other martial arts, kickboxing follows a progressive grading system. It takes about three years of dedicated training for a kickboxer to attain a black belt. A novice kickboxer starts with a white belt and, through ongoing training, progresses to yellow, orange, green, blue, purple and brown belts, finally achieving the prized black belt. The kickboxing student grades when his instructor decides that he is sufficiently ready and prepared for the 'examination'.

In kickboxing gradings you are judged mostly on your physical fitness and conditioning, your fighting ability, as well as your technique and style. You must at all times show tremendous fighting spirit and show that you fear nothing during your grading.

The kickboxer on the left has just landed a left jab to the opponent's body during a sparring session, while the grading master, who is controlling the session, carefully looks on. Sparring focus is an important part of grading — to attain your black belt you have to do 10 rounds of sparring.

The role of the kickboxing trainer

How to choose a trainer

It is important that you are coached by an experienced, professional trainer. Your trainer will spend as much time in the gym as you and is at all times motivating and spurring you on to greater efforts and achievements. He is also your mentor and ensures that your mental attitude is positive and that you are focused on attaining your kickboxing goals. At the same time your trainer has to plan your training programme, work out your diet and see that you maintain a disciplined lifestyle in order to become a kickboxing champion.

Taking all of this into consideration, it is important that you choose a trainer who has a successful track record and with whom you can cultivate a good, lasting relationship.

above THE KICKBOXER IS PRACTISING AN ELBOW STRIKE TO THE THAI PAD HELD BY THE TRAINER. PRACTISING YOUR TECHNIQUES AGAINST THAI PADS DEVELOPS YOUR POWER, SPEED AND TIMING.
left THE KICKBOXER IS DELIVERING A LEFT ROUNDHOUSE KICK TO THE HEAD AGAINST THE THAI PADS. TECHNIQUES LIKE THIS ARE PRACTISED REPEATEDLY EVERY DAY TO PERFECT AND DEVELOP THE POWER IN YOUR PUNCHES AND KICKS.

Ringcraft & tactics

Ringcraft refers to your all-round ability, knowledge, skill and understanding of the fight game. A kickboxer builds this largely through experience and the guidance and teachings of his trainer or coach.

Tactics refers to the game-plan you employ in order to defeat a particular opponent. In partnership with your coach, you need to study your opponent's style of fighting, as well as his strengths and weaknesses, before deciding on the best tactics to employ in order to beat him.

If you are a professional kickboxer preparing for a national, international or world title fight, your trainer will get all the video material of your opponent's previous fights and all other relevant information concerning him. Together you can decide on the best game plan and tactics to adopt in order to defeat your opponent.

Tactics against kickboxers of different styles

Fighting against a 'southpaw'

A southpaw is a kickboxer who fights from a right fighting stance, as opposed to the more conventional left fighting stance. To prepare yourself before fighting a southpaw you need to spar against sparring partners who are good, natural southpaws.

The best way to fight a southpaw is to counter his attacks with strong right crosses to the head, as well as using powerful right roundhouses and front kicks to his body. Another tactic to adopt against a southpaw is to fight from a southpaw stance yourself. A warning: only do this if you have sufficient confidence and ability to fight in this way.

As your own left jab will be largely negated against a southpaw, you should feint with your left and then attack with right punches to his body and head, following this up with other combinations of punches and kicks.

Fighting against an expert kicker

To fight an opponent who is an exceptional kicker you must move in and block or jam his kicks, thus throwing him off balance. You can then counter with punches to his head and body.

If it is a low kick or Thai boxing bout you can move in and counter his own kicks with low kicks to his legs. This is particularly effective against high kicks, as your opponent will be supporting himself on one leg. Countering with your own low kick to that leg will prove highly effective.

You should put pressure on a good kicker by moving forward to attack him with strong punches and kicks at every opportunity. Never let him dictate the fight and get you in a position where you are vulnerable to him launching dangerous kicks. You must pressure a good kicker at all times.

Fighting a dangerous puncher or boxer

A kickboxer who has a big punch is a constant danger because he is capable of knocking you out at any time, even during the final seconds of the bout. To fight a dangerous puncher, or a kickboxer who comes from a boxing background, do not try to slug it out with him. Rather use your left jab as your main weapon, which should prevent him from coming in at you. Use strong left front kicks to his midsection as he launches an attack, as this will both discourage him and pile up points for you.

Another tactic you can employ against a big puncher is to try and keep him at long range by using side kicks, front kicks and spinning back kicks to force him to keep his distance from you. This should frustrate him and cause him to get careless, thereby setting himself up for your assault with strong punching combinations.

Another tactic you can adopt is to move constantly around the ring and successfully employ evasion techniques. You can then counter your opponent each time you evade his attacks.

Fighting a tall opponent with a long reach

To fight a kickboxer who is taller than you and who has a longer reach, you must slip inside his attacks and counter with combination punches to his body and head. If he attacks with a long range kick to your head, move in and block his kick, which should cause him to lose his balance. You can then counter with your own strong punches.

A KICKBOXER'S HANDS MUST BE PROPERLY TAPED IN ORDER TO CONFORM TO THE RULES OF KICKBOXING.

Another tactic you can use against a tall opponent is to attack his body with strong front leg side kicks, following this with a fast spinning back fist to his head. You can also use the side kick when he steps in to attack you with straight punches.

If you are a strong and aggressive fighter, you can pressurize a taller opponent by continually moving forward and attacking his body with combination punches, before switching your attack to his head, the most vulnerable area for a knockout.

Fighting against a spoiler

A spoiler is a kickboxer who uses negative and foul tactics to rough you up and intimidate you. He does this to mentally unbalance you as well as to physically intimidate you. A spoiler can make the best kickboxer look bad and will use head butts, elbows, illegal holding, pushing and swearing as part of his spoiling tactics.

Whatever you do, do not lose your cool against a spoiler. Remain calm and use your skill, ability and ringcraft to out-think and out-manoeuvre him. Stick to the basics and follow your trainer's instructions between rounds, as he will be the best judge as to what tactics and strategies you should adopt.

Fighting an opponent who is your equal

When fighting someone who is your equal in every way, you will have to call upon all your experience, know-how and expertise in order to defeat him.

As your trainer will always tell you, try to command the centre of the ring. Try to out-jab your opponent, which will set up kicking and punching attacks from behind your jab. It's important to maintain a high work-rate in every round against such an opponent. Feint and use all your deceptive tricks in order to out-think him.

All things being equal, in such an encounter the fighter who has the strongest will, spirit and sustained concentration will emerge as the winner.

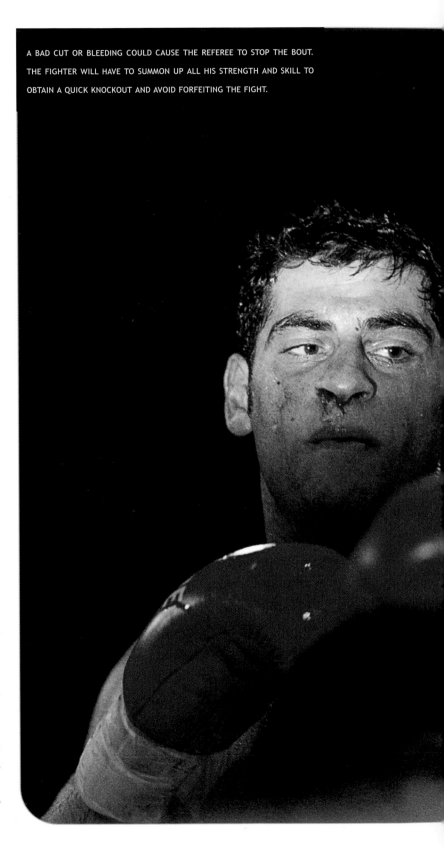

A BAD CUT OR BLEEDING COULD CAUSE THE REFEREE TO STOP THE BOUT. THE FIGHTER WILL HAVE TO SUMMON UP ALL HIS STRENGTH AND SKILL TO OBTAIN A QUICK KNOCKOUT AND AVOID FORFEITING THE FIGHT.

Improving ringcraft and tactical skills

Defence is important in kickboxing. Never take a punch or a kick if you can avoid it by either blocking, parrying or evading. You must also always counterattack immediately after defending your opponent's own attack. Your counterattacks must always be strong and aggressive. Ask no quarter, and give none in return.

My own philosophy in kickboxing is that there is no forestalling in fighting — you strike your opponent when or before he strikes you. I am also a great believer that attack is the best form of defence; therefore, your defence must be strong, aggressive and effective.

Mastering the left jab

You must train yourself assiduously to develop a strong left jab. The left jab should be developed as an attacking technique. You must execute the left jab with speed and power. If you do not put maximum power and force into your jab you will not be able to strike your opponent and stop him in his tracks when he launches an attack. Practise the jab by putting your weight on your left leg and stepping forward with your full body weight as you throw the left jab.

Most kickboxers' left jabs are ineffective and, in fact, are little more than powder-puff punches. You can usually walk right through most kickboxers' jabs and attack with your own power punches and kicks. Your opponents might well try this against you, which is another reason why you should strengthen your own jabs in order to reduce your opponent's attacking options against you.

Never try to knock out your opponent

You should never enter the ring with the intention of knocking out your opponent. A knockout happens during a bout when you either outfight your opponent or else wear him down with sustained combination attacks, thereby setting him up for the knockout.

From the first round you should only be concerned with outfighting your opponent by using all your skills, power, speed and know-how. Out-think and out-fight your opponent and you will win the fight, either by points or by a knockout.

Another important aspect in kickboxing is that you must always punch or kick with power. Put your entire weight behind your punches and kicks — the harder you punch or kick the more toll it will take on your opponent, causing him to become flustered or to drop his guard, thus allowing you to set him up for the big KO punch or kick.

How to deal with injuries in the ring

If you are injured during a kickboxing bout you must do everything in your power to conceal the effects of your injury from your opponent. Under no circumstances should you let him know that your fighting ability has been impaired in any way.

If you have been rocked by a powerful punch or kick you should go into a clinch and hold your opponent until you have had time to recover. Do this several times if necessary.

If you are knocked down at any stage during a bout you should stay down until the count of eight, and only then get up, again to make the most of the break. If you have not fully recovered by then, go into a clinch to prevent your opponent from attacking you.

You might incur a bad cut during a bout which could convince the referee to consider stopping the fight. If this happens you will have to call on all your power, cunning and experience to try and knock your opponent out before the referee decides to stop the fight.

Final thoughts

In concluding, I would like to offer the following advice to young kickboxers — cultivate your kickboxing skills, train hard and develop explosive power in your punches and kicks. Punching and kicking an opponent hard saps his energy and weakens his resistance, thereby setting up a victory possibility for you. Work on your speed and always maintain good balance. Practise your combinations of punches and kicks so that you can deliver them with pinpoint accuracy and land them with speed and explosive power. Finally, utilize aggressive defence as part of your tactics by countering your opponent's attacks with powerful, fast and accurate punches and kicks of your own.

KICKBOXING IN DEFENCE

The philosophy and teachings of kickboxing are similar to those of other martial arts. The aim is to learn how to fight successfully, while practising restraint and self-control outside the ring and not use your fighting skills except when you are driven to so and are acting in self-defence.

It must, however, be realized that kickboxing is a potentially lethal sport, and that its aims and the attitudes of instructors are serious. Your trainer's duty is to teach you the techniques that will allow you to defend and protect yourself whether you are facing an opponent in the ring or on the street.

An instructor's aim is to develop in his students the 'warrior attitude', which is to be brave, courageous and fearless. He has to instil these mental traits in his students' minds in order to prepare them for combat situations, both in and out of the ring.

Kickboxing is incredibly practical and effective. What you have learned, even in your very first training class, can be applied immediately. Gradually, you are taught how to jab and deliver a straight cross, how to hook and deliver an uppercut. You will learn how to use low kicks, elbow and knee strikes, all of them powerful and useful techniques. You'll become familiar with throws, takedown techniques and groundwork, arm locks as well as leg and foot submission holds. These techniques, taught to beginners, are exactly the same as those used by professional fighters.

There are no secrets in kickboxing: it is a combative martial art that has the potential to do lethal harm. All the techniques have been tried, tested and proven to be completely effective in actual combat situations.

You don't have to become a professional kickboxer or even a world champion in order to become a good kickboxer. You can train at your own pace and to your own level of commitment, but even so, within a short period of time you will be able to defend yourself if you are attacked.

In an attack situation a fighting spirit or 'killer instinct' is needed to survive, as criminals do not adhere to any rules. Please note, however, that while kickboxing teaches useful self-defence techniques as well as improving strength and agility, only experienced exponents of the sport should attempt to defend themselves against weapon-wielding attackers.

Some mental attributes you need to cultivate to become a good fighter in actual attack situations

- Be aware of your surroundings at all times
- Become an explosive puncher, kicker and grappler
- Stay calm and relaxed under all circumstances
- Stay focused and think clearly at all times
- Never assume anything
- There are no rules (on the street)
- Do whatever you have to do in order to win
- Be deceptive and fast
- Endure punishment and overcome pain
- Be confident and determined
- Expect anything
- Be brave, courageous and a fearless warrior

Develop these traits and enshrine them in your heart and mind and then you will become a fighter who will be hard to beat under any circumstances.

A top-class kickboxer or fighter chooses the fighting techniques that will be most effective based on the distance between him and his opponent. The different combat ranges are: punching and kicking range, knee,

opposite THE ABILITY TO REMAIN FOCUSED, AS WELL AS CALM AND RELAXED, IS ESSENTIAL FOR SUCCESS IN KICKBOXING.

elbow and head strike range, and throwing and grappling range. You should always utilize your best and most effective combinations and techniques depending on the range you find yourself in during combat.

If you follow all the training techniques and programmes outlined in this book, and if you can master all the basic techniques and combinations, you will become a good kickboxer after only six months of training. Be sincere, train hard and regularly and strive to develop a warrior's attitude. Be brave, courageous and fearless — this should become your mantra (or affirmation) as a kickboxer.

As a kickboxer you are taught the same values and code of ethics as in any other martial art; principles such as self-control, discipline, respect for others, etiquette and a positive mental attitude. Kickboxers are taught to control their minds and to remain calm at all times while competing. Furthermore, a kickboxer must refrain from any acts of aggression or violence towards anyone, except in dire situations where he is forced to defend himself or others from being attacked by one or more assailants.

The ultimate aim and the spiritual perspective of kickboxing is the unification of body, mind and spirit. To attain this you have to empty your mind of all thoughts and emotions originating from fear, all sense of insecurity and all desire to win. The warrior who can achieve this unification of body-mind-spirit becomes invincible. This is because the movements of his opponent will be reflected in his own mind without thought. His mind has become still through constant practise and meditation and will respond to the thousand situations but remains ever still within. The art culminates here. Nothing else remains to be done.

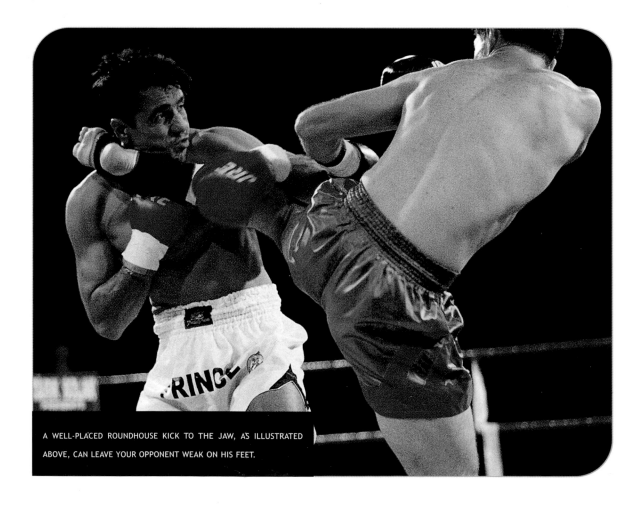

A WELL-PLACED ROUNDHOUSE KICK TO THE JAW, AS ILLUSTRATED ABOVE, CAN LEAVE YOUR OPPONENT WEAK ON HIS FEET.

Self-defence against punches and kicks on the street

Defence against a left jab to the face

As your assailant throws a left jab to your face, step to the side, block and grab his left wrist, counter with your own right cross, and then take him down with a right footsweep. When he hits the floor deliver another punch and then apply an arm lock.

Defence against a right punch to the face

Block your opponent's right arm with your left palm, counter with a right elbow strike to his face followed by a right knee to his solar plexus as you grab him around his neck and pull him down. Finally, deliver a right downward elbow strike to the back of his head.

Defence against a right punch to the head

The attacker prepares to attack (A), and as he throws a right punch to the defender's head it is blocked with an inside forearm block (B). The defender delivers a strong front kick with her shin to the attacker's groin (C), and finishes her attacker off by pulling him down and executing a knee strike to his solar plexus (D).

Defence against a left front kick to the body

Block and deflect your opponent's left front kick with your left arm and counter with your own left roundhouse to his head. Finally, throw your opponent.

Defence against a right roundhouse kick to the head

Block and grab your assailant's right kick to your head counter with a knee kick to his groin, then throw him to the ground by sweeping his left leg. Finish off the technique by executing a stamping kick to your assailant's groin.

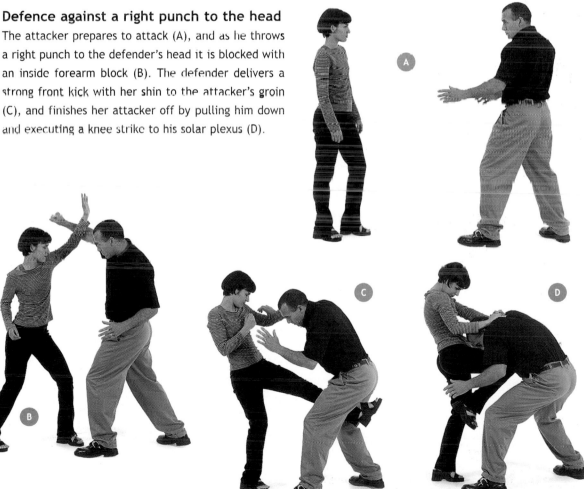

Defence against attack from the rear

Attacker grabs the defender from the rear in a bear hug around her arms and body (A). The defender steps with her right leg to the side to create the necessary space and then strikes the attacker with a knife hand strike to his groin (B). Defender then strikes the attacker's arms upwards (C), then bends down, grabs his ankle with both hands and jerks his leg upwards, thereby throwing him backwards (D). The defender then steps over with her right leg while holding onto the attacker's own leg (E). She then delivers a down stomping kick to his groin (F).

Defence against two attackers

Two attackers line themselves up to attack the defender (A). The attacker in front attacks with a left jab to the body, which the defender blocks with a palm heel block and simultaneously counters with a strong front kick to his solar plexus (B), which should knock the attacker down. As the second attacker launches his attack by throwing a right punch, the defender executes a back kick to his body (C).

Defence against three attackers surrounding you

As assailant one attacks with a right punch to the body, block and counter with a punch to his head (B). Then pivot and block assailant two's right punch (C), countering with a right roundhouse to his body (D). Finally, kick assailant three with a left side kick as he moves in to grab you (E).

If you have to deal with multiple attackers, try to remain calm and sum up the situation as best you can. Attacks happen fast as they nearly always rely on the surprise element. You should find, however, that your training will assist you and you will be better equipped to defend yourself in such a situation.

Defence against an assailant with a knife

Straight thrust to the head

Deflect and then grab your assailant's arm as he attempts a straight thrust to your head (B). Counter with a side thrust kick to his ribs (C), put your opponent's arm into an arm lock (D) and then deliver an elbow strike to his head (E). After applying a wrist lock on your opponent, apply pressure and force him to the ground (F). You can then take the knife from him and hold it to his throat to force him into submission.

> *Only highly experienced kickboxers should attempt to fight off one or more attackers who are armed with a weapon.*

Defence against an assailant with a pistol
Frontal hold up with a pistol

If an assailant holds you at bay by pointing a pistol at you from a frontal position (A), kick the gun out of his hand with a crescent kick (B) and then pivot and kick him in the solar plexus, or the face, with a spinning back kick (C). To finally disable him, grab him by his neck with both hands and pull his face down and deliver a knee strike to his face (D).

Only highly experienced kickboxers should attempt to fight off one or more attackers who are armed with a weapon.

Hold up from the rear by an assailant with a pistol

If you are held up by an assailant jabbing a pistol into your back (A), pivot on your right foot at 45 degrees, block and then grab his wrist (B), before countering with a left elbow to his face (C). Apply a wrist lock (D), from where you can take his weapon from him as you wrestle him to the ground (E) and hold him captive with his pistol (F).

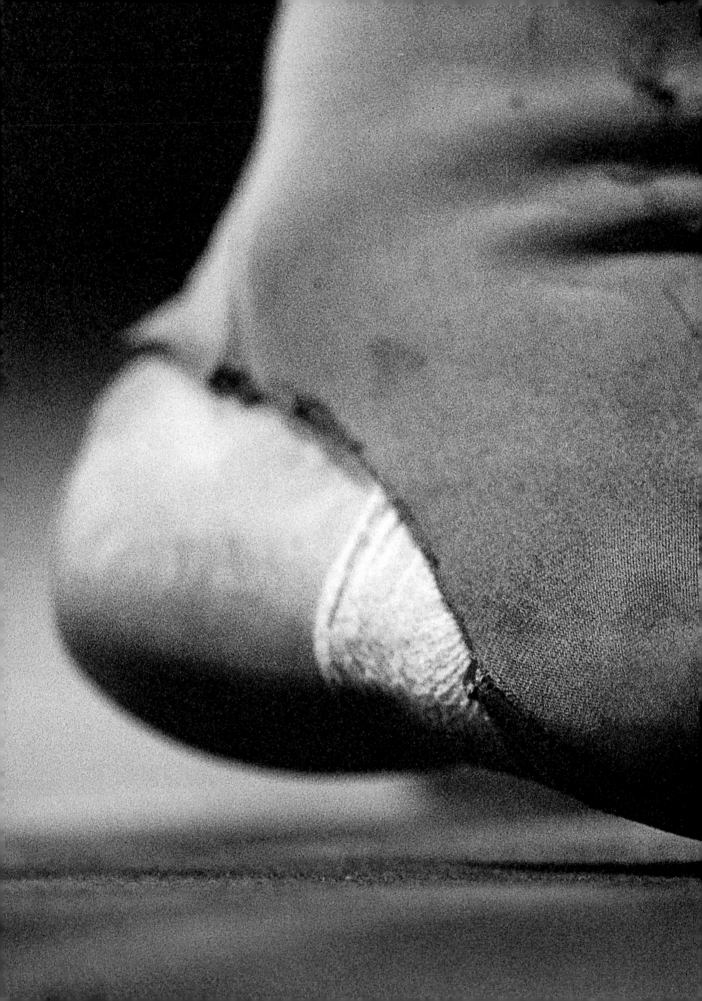

MAKING CONTACT

Professional and national kickboxing associations are usually staffed by experienced kickboxing trainers who have considerable insight into training and techniques for most levels of kickboxing, and can offer sound advice and guidance as well as assisting you with grading and entering kickboxing competitions.

INTERNATIONAL KICKBOXING ASSOCIATIONS

WAKO — WORLD ASSOCIATION OF KICKBOXING ORGANIZATIONS
- WAKO Headquarters
- Via Francesco Algarotti 4, 20124, Milan, Italy
- Tel: (2) 67 077 030
- Fax: (2) 67 070 474
- Website: www.wako-fikeda.it
- E-mail: info@wako-fikeda.it

WKA — WORLD KICKBOXING ASSOCIATION
- WAK Head Office
- James Court, 63 Gravely Lane, Erdington, Birmingham B23 6LX, England
- Tel: (0) 121 382 2995
- Fax: (0) 121 382 5688
- Website: www.wka.co.uk
- E-mail: info@wka.co.uk

- WAK USA
- Website: www.wkausa.com

ISKA — INTERNATIONAL SPORT KICKBOXING ASSOCIATION
- World Headquarters
- Post Office Box 90147, Gainesville, Florida 32607-0147, USA
- Tel: (352) 374 6876
- Fax: (352) 378 4454
- Website: www.iska.com

IKF — INTERNATIONAL KICKBOXING FEDERATION
- 9385 Old State Highway, PO Box 1205, Newcastle, CA 95658, USA
- Tel: (916) 663 2467
- Fax: (916) 663 4510
- Website: www.ikfkickboxing.com
- E-mail: ikf@jps.net

GLOSSARY

Axe kick kick executed from above to land on opponent's head or chest

Back fist strike delivered with back of gloved hand

Bag work practising punches/kicks on a punch- or speed bag

Blocking preventing an opponent's punches/kicks from landing, by blocking with hands, forearms and knees

Bobbing ducking under punch or kick

Combination punches succession of punches to weaken opponent

Dodging evasive body movement

Downward elbow strike elbow strike to back or top of opponent's head

Elbow strike any strike using elbow

empty-hand any martial art combat (such as karate) without weapons

Fighting stance alert stance assumed when ready to begin fighting

Floor-to-ceiling ball small punchbag suspended on elastic rope; used to sharpen reflexes and eyesight

Focus pad training implement used to practise punches

Footwork steps forward, backward and sideways to attack or evade

Front elbow strike same as a punch, but landing with elbow instead of fist

Front kick fast kick delivered by raising the knee and kicking foot straight into opponent

Front knee kick forward strike with knee, often delivered after grabbing opponent around the neck and pulling down (allowed in Muay Thai bouts)

Full-contact bouts in boxing ring; target area strictly above the belt

grading evaluation of a student's progress and award of higher grade (belt) to successful candidates

Hook kick circular kick in opposite direction to roundhouse kick

Hook (left or right) powerful knock-out punch with bent elbow held away from the body

Jab straight, quick, sharp strike with extended arm

Jumping front kick leaping up to deliver a front kick, both feet off the floor (surprise attack)

Jumping knee kick knee kick while leaping up

Jumping side kick side kick while leaping up

Kama traditional Okinawan weapon

Knee kick blow to opponent's body, delivered with the knee

Knock out (KO) boxer unable to get up within 10-count knockdown rule

Light-contact (continuous fighting) punches/kicks strictly above the belt; fight not stopped when point is scored

Low kick (outside and inside) kicks delivered to in- or outside of opponent's thigh

Muay Thai Thai boxing (use of knees, elbows, low kicks and throws allowed during bouts)

Mushin Japanese word, 'empty mind'

Musical form choreographed martial art sequence set to music

Parrying deflecting punches/kicks with hands, elbows or forearms

Pear bag (see Speed bag)

Range distance from opponent

Right Cross right hand punch thrown over opponent's left jab

Ringcraft a fighter's overall ability

Roundhouse kick (front and rear) kick delivered to opponent's head

Sai traditional Okinawan weapon

Semi-contact punches/kicks strictly above the belt; fight stopped every time a point is scored

Shadow sparring fighting against an imaginary opponent

Shovel hook (left or right) close-range punch halfway between a hook and an uppercut

Side elbow strike sideway strike with elbow, usually from on-guard position

Side knee kick kick delivered in roundhouse motion

Slipping evasive left or right movement to avoid punch/kick to head

Southpaw left-handed fighter

Sparring practise round between two kickboxers

Speed bag training implement used to sharpen reflexes, speed and timing

Spinning kicks all spinning kicks are executed by pivoting the body 180 degrees from the original stance

Stance standing position of a fighter

Sweeping (outside and inside) foot movement to opponent's leg

Technical knock-out (TKO) referee stops bout when one fighter is clearly disadvantaged, or has been knocked down more than three times

Thai pad pads strapped onto trainer's forearms to allow student to practise kicks, elbow- and knee strikes

Thrust kick front or side kick with leg thrust out fully extended

Tonfa traditional Okinawan weapon

Uppercut (left or right) punch executed in upward motion

Weaving evasive left or right movement to avoid punch/kick to head

Whai Kru ceremony that introduces traditional Thai boxing bouts

INDEX

PHOTOGRAPHIC CREDITS

All cover photography by Ryno Reyneke. All other photography by Ryno Reyneke with the exception of those supplied by photographers and/or agencies as listed below. Key to photographers (Copyright rests with the following photographers and/or their agents): AS=Allsport; C=Corbis; GS=Great Stock; TSI/GI=Tony Stone Images/Gallo Images.

Endpapers	TSI/GI		62	GS
2	C		64-65	TSI/GI
3—4	C		67	C
6	AS		69	AS
8	AS		73	C
9-10	AS		77	TSI/GI
13	GS		78	AS
14	AS		80	C
15	AS		81	TSI/GI
46	AS		82	AS
47	AS		90—91	AS
56	TSI/GI		96	AS